The First Americans
Prehistory–1600

TEACHING GUIDE FOR THE
REVISED 3RD EDITION

For Elementary School Classes

OXFORD
UNIVERSITY PRESS

Oxford University Press
Oxford   New York
Auckland   Bangkok   Buenos Aires
Cape Town   Chennai   Dar es Salaam   Delhi   Hong Kong   Istanbul
Karachi   Kolkata   Kuala Lumpur   Madrid   Melbourne   Mexico City   Mumbai
Nairobi   São Paulo   Shanghai   Singapore   Taipei   Tokyo   Toronto

and an associated company
Berlin

Copyright © 2003 by Oxford University Press, Inc.

Published by Oxford University Press, Inc.
198 Madison Avenue, New York, New York 10016
Oxford is a registered trademark of Oxford University Press

ISBN 978-019-976734-2

Writer: Karen Edwards
Editor: Rosely Himmelstein
Editorial Consultant: Susan Buckley

Printed in the United States of America on acid-free paper

CONTENTS

NOTE FROM THE AUTHOR

Dear Teacher,

Every writer of history has to make decisions. Most of those decisions are about what to leave out. It would take libraries and libraries of books to include all of America's history (and there would still be things left out).

So there are all kinds of stories about America (and its heroes and villains and ordinary people) that are not in this book. I see that as an opportunity for you and your students. Tell them the author is upset about what she had to omit. Have them do their own chapters of *A History of US*. Maybe you can do a class volume. Consider focusing on family stories: what can each of your students find out about his or her ancestors? Or maybe you'll want to do a book about your community with chapters on people and organizations and past events.

I have fun tracking down stories; I think you and your students will, too. (Yes, I hope you'll become a student with them.) Writing history is a lot like being a detective or a newspaper reporter. It involves searching for information, digesting it, and then using it. There are hardly any better skills for this Information Age of ours.

You and your students might want to find out more about Indians—especially the Native Americans in the region where you live. Or more about Coronado, or Ben Franklin, or about Americans not even mentioned in these books. Good writers look for details. Check paintings and photographs. What does your subject look like? How did he or she dress? What was daily life like for that person?

You might want to produce the work in comic book form, or write it as a play, or create a ballad. The big idea here is to "do" history, as you might do art or music. At its best, it's a creative activity.

But the big reason I wrote these books was to teach reading and, when it comes to critical reading, history shines. Few subjects give you real events and real people to discuss and analyze. Literacy exercises and paragraph analysis may help some students, but there is nothing like reading a whole book—tracing its ideas from chapter to chapter, and then talking about the ideas—to make a mind work.

This learning guide has words to study and maps to look at and questions to answer. You may want your students to do all the activities, or you may want them to do just a few. Some activities are for those who want to go beyond the text.

Will all this help students pass standardized tests? You bet. Just to be sure, though, I have added some pages with names and dates that you may ask students to memorize.

But there are things in history more important than memorized dates. History is a thinking subject, and you have Information Age kids as your charge. Doing history means reading, researching, finding information, and making connections. If you want to stretch young minds, history will make it happen.

Joy Hakim

ABOUT THIS TEACHING GUIDE

A History of US is the story of what happened in the United States to the people who live here—both before and after the country got its name. In *The First Americans*, students will learn what happened in America from prehistoric times through 1600. This teaching guide, containing strategies and assessment suggestions as well as a range of activities for enrichment and extension, was prepared to help you guide your students through the book.

FOCUSING ON FREEDOM

The cornerstone of American history is Freedom. It is the idea that pulsates throughout *A History of US:* the hunger for freedom, the fight for freedom, the legislating of freedom, the protection of freedom, the defense of freedom. As you teach this volume of *A History of US,* students will learn how the accomplishments of people, the force of ideas, and the outcome of events are all linked in this nation's great story of Freedom.

A lot happens: sad, exhilarating, unexpected, disappointing, terrible, puzzling, inspiring things. And many people are involved: the wise, the misguided, the brave, the reckless, the patient, the bullies, the compromisers. It's a grand and sweeping story.

May you and your students enjoy it together.

THE TEACHING UNITS

Each book of *A History of US* has been divided into units of study that we call Parts. Each Part consists of chapters that have a common focus. The Teaching Guide provides strategies and activities that you can use to teach each Part.

- **Part 1: Beginning the Journey** (Chapters 1-4) focuses on the movement of the first peoples from Siberia to the Americas.

- **Part 2: Adapting to a Diverse Land** (Chapters 5-12) focuses on the diversity of Native American cultures.

- **Part 3: Expanding European Horizons** (Chapters 13-20) focuses on the European exploration of the Americas.

- **Part 4: Clash of Cultures** (Chapters 21-24) focuses on the conflicts caused by the establishment of New Spain.

- **Part 5: The March North** (Chapters 25-29) focuses on Spanish explorations from Florida to California in the 1500s.

- **Part 6: Enter the French** (Chapters 30-34) focuses on the events that led the French to challenge Spanish control of North America.

- **Part 7: Enter the English** (Chapters 35-39) focuses on England's plans to build an empire in North America.

ORGANIZING INFORMATION

The history of the United States is rich, busy, and populated. You can help your students organize information and reinforce learning by frequently asking these questions:

- What were the major events?

- Who were the significant people?

- What were the important ideas?

✔ **Question Chart** In every lesson plan, you will see a reference to the Question Chart (Resource 1, TG page 72), on which students may record their answers to these questions as they progress through the book.

THE BIG THEMES

Underlying the events and people and ideas that enliven this series are certain themes—themes that run through human experience and help us make sense of the past.

Among these themes are Justice, Conflict, Independence, Change, Diversity, Adaptation, Growth, and Power. You may wish to post these themes on the walls of your classroom and refer to them at appropriate times. They may also stir students' thinking throughout the course of their study.

Book 1 of *A History of US* focuses on three Big Themes: **Movement, Adaptation,** and **Diversity.** These themes—and how they relate to this nation's early quest for freedom—provide the conceptual framework of *The First Americans.*

Among the major movements in the period discussed in this book are:

- movement of people from Siberia to the Americas during the Ice Age.

- movement of the First Americans throughout the continents.

- movement of Spanish, French, and English to the Americas.

Among the adaptations in the period are:

- adaptation to new environments by the First Americans, Native Americans, and Europeans.

- adaptation to new ideas by America's inhabitants.

Among the examples of diversity in the period are:

- differences among the Native American cultures and the racial and ethnic groups in the Americas.

- diversity of religious beliefs, social structures, and governments among the inhabitants.

TEACHING STRATEGIES

The Teaching Strategies in this guide are organized in the following manner:

Introducing the Part lays out goals for teaching, sets up a relationship between the Part and the major themes, and seeks to stimulate students' interest as they begin to read the text.

Chapter Lesson Plans are designed to provide you with the flexibility that your individual schedule, interests, and students' abilities may require. You may choose from the following categories:

- **Ask:** straightforward questions to elicit from your students responses that demonstrate their recall and understanding of the text.

- **Discuss:** critical thinking questions to stimulate classroom and/or small-group discussions.

- **Write:** topics for classroom or homework assignment, allowing students to express their comprehension or impressions of the chapter's events, ideas, or people.

- **Ponder:** questions that give students the opportunity to reflect on the thematic material of the chapter, often relating it to their own lives.

- **Literacy Links:** *Words to Discuss,* exploring the chapter's significant vocabulary words or terms, and *Reading Skills* designed to help students develop reading skills, especially for reading nonfiction.

- **Skills Connection:** chapter-related activities to strengthen geography skills, chart/graph skills, study skills, and cross-curricula skills.

- **Meeting Individual Needs:** activities that address the needs of students with differing learning abilities.

Which of these categories will be suitable for your students on any particular day? How many items will be useful to engage your class—or a particular student? The lesson plans have been structured with the belief that *you* are the best person to make these decisions.

Summarizing the Part provides guidance for synthesizing the Part's Big Themes. This guidance consists of a series of questions—which you can use for assessment or discussion—that enable students to deepen their understanding of how the events, ideas, trends, and personalities of the Part reflect common themes. The Part Summary also provides additional Projects and Activities.

PART CHECK-UPS

The reproducible Check-Ups review the content of each Part.

RESOURCES

The Resources are reproducible blackline masters. They cover social studies skills (including maps, graphic organizers, tables, primary sources, and other enrichment materials), critical thinking skills, and reading comprehension skills.

LITERACY AND *A HISTORY OF US*

In our Information Age, reading is an essential survival skill. So what does this have to do with us historians and history educators? We have the key to the nation's reading crisis, and we've been ignoring it: When it comes to critical reading, history shines. Hardly anything approaches it in its demands for analysis and thinking.
Joy Hakim

Teaching with *A History of US* gives you an unparalleled opportunity to focus on literacy. As the author has noted, "Nonfiction is the literary form of our time." Joy Hakim's highly readable nonfiction is a unique tool for teaching strategic reading skills.

READING STRATEGIES AND SKILLS

In order to help your students get the most out of their reading, the Teaching Guides include activities that focus on reading skills as well as reading strategies.

Reading Skills deal with what students actively do with the nonfiction text. The Reading Skills activities in the chapter lesson plans help students identify, evaluate, interpret, understand, and use the following nonfiction elements:

- Text Structure: main idea/supporting details, sequence, comparing and contrasting, question and answer, cause and effect

- Text Features: margin notes, special sections, captions, headings, typeface

- Visual Aids: photographs, paintings, illustrations, political cartoons

- Graphic Aids: graphs, tables, charts, timelines

- Maps: political, physical, historical, special purpose

- Point of View: author's voice and opinion

- Source Material: primary and secondary sources

- Rhetorical Devices: word choice, imagery, connotation/denotation, persuasion, fact and opinion, analogy

Reading Strategies are the intellectual strategies necessary for readers to use their reading skills. Following the ideas of reading authority Janet Allen, these can be categorized as follows:

- Questioning: creating questions to aid with previewing, recalling, and deeper understanding of the text

- Predicting: focusing and guiding reading by previewing text elements and posing questions to be answered

- Visualizing: identifying and using language and imagery to infer, make connections to the text, and predict

- Inferring: identifying text clues and background knowledge to make inferences; using inferences to make predictions and draw conclusions

- Connecting: making personal connections to the text, seeing connections between texts, seeing connections between world events and the text

- Analyzing: recognizing the relationship between author's intention and author's words, determining author's purpose, understanding how parts of the text work together, using material from the text to support response to the text

- Synthesizing: creating an original idea, new line of thinking, or other new creation by combining related ideas

Each Reading Skill activity is related to one of the Reading Strategy categories.

NOTE You probably present material to your students in a variety of ways. There are times you may read aloud to the class or in small groups. Perhaps you'll find it best to have volunteers read aloud—or have the class read silently. You'll find that *A History of US* allows you to vary your approach to suit your schedule and your goals.

LITERACY HANDBOOK: *READING HISTORY*

Reading History is written by Janet Allen, one of American's most prominent literacy advocates. Engaged in the blossoming campaign to integrate literacy and history, Allen provides valuable strategies for teaching nonfiction, taking all examples directly from *A History of US*. Allen says:

> *For the past several years, many content teachers have voiced a common complaint: As we teach and learn with a generation of children who have been raised on technology and sophisticated media, it becomes increasingly difficult to entice them into reading content textbooks.* Reading History *has been written to help you teach your students effective strategies for reading* A History of US *as well as other nonfiction. It is filled with practical ideas for making reading history accessible for even your most reluctant readers.*

ASSESSMENT AND *A HISTORY OF US*

Author Joy Hakim intentionally omits from her books the kinds of section, chapter, and unit questions that are used to review and assess learning in standard textbooks. It is her purpose to engage readers in learning—and loving—history. Rather than interrupt student reading, all assessment instruments for *A History of US* appear in the Teaching Guides.

IN THE TEACHING GUIDES

Ask, Discuss, and Write sections in each chapter lesson plan check students' understanding of chapter content.

Summarizing the Part includes questions for discussion or writing, and activities that help students identify major concepts and themes.

Check-Up pages review content for each Part. These are reproducible pages that appear at the end of each Teaching Guide.

HISTORICAL OVERVIEW

Balboa reaches the Pacific Ocean.

What is dramatic to our age may seem mundane to the next. While the best history has enduring elements, there is a sense in which every generation has to have history rewritten for it.
—Allan Nevins, The Gateway to History

Allan Nevins, the distinguished American historian, believed that change was one of the few constants in history. Our own approach to United States history is an example of how a generation can "refocus" its lenses to examine the past from a fresh perspective.

Not so long ago, most history books began the story of our nation with the first successful English settlements in the early 1600s. Today we realize that the English were in fact latecomers. Ancestors of the Native Americans preceded them by tens of thousands of years. The Spaniards also explored the Americas long before the English. So did the enslaved Africans, dragged across the Atlantic in chains by Spanish and Portuguese slave traders.

The most important fact about our history is this: the ancestors of anybody who calls himself or herself an American came from someplace else. We are, declares a popular saying, a nation of immigrants. Historians now start the story of our immigrant nation with the Native Americans Their forebears were the first wave of peoples to wash over our land. Archaeologists debate their arrival time. (Estimates vary from 10,000 to more than 100,000 years ago.) But a trail of artifacts from the Yukon to Patagonia attests to their early presence.

The diversity and sophistication of human cultures in the Americas rivaled that of early peoples elsewhere in the world. No longer do historians view Native American cultures with the ethnocentric eye of earlier generations. The achievements of Native Americans speak for themselves: invention of farming in Mesoamerica; systems of writing by the Maya and Aztec; architectural wonders in Chaco Canyon, New Mexico; creation of a federation of Iroquois nations; beautiful artistic works and complex spiritual beliefs of peoples throughout the Americas.

Against the long histories and accomplishments of Native Americans, European expressions such as "discovery of the Americas" or "New World" sound hollow. But, early explorers had shattered European world views, and when the Europeans first reached the Americas, the land did seem new to them.

In the 16th century, idealistic dreams mixed with national pride and greed as the Europeans marched into the Americas. First the Spaniards, then the French, and finally the English carried their customs and beliefs across the Atlantic. In the Americas, however, peoples adapted not only to the land but to one another. More importantly, the movement of goods and peoples among four continents—Europe, Africa, and North and South America—opened the way to today's diverse world.

Book One traces the early paths to and across the Americas. Each of the seven parts recommended for teaching the book serves as a "roadmarker" on the journey.

Magellen, whose expedition sailed around the world.

TEACHING STRATEGIES FOR BOOK ONE

Beginning the Journey

In the mid-1500s, the Spanish priest Bartolomé de Las Casas was amazed by the diversity of peoples he saw on islands in the Caribbean and in present-day Mexico and Central America. Las Casas rightly concluded that "the people of these islands and continent are . . . very ancient." Part 1 tells about the journey of the First Americans—the first humans to inhabit America's lands and adapt to its resources.

SETTING GOALS

The goals for students in Part 1 are to:
- understand what history is, and how and why it is studied.
- describe the effects that geography and climate had on the first humans to come to the Americas.
- understand how the First Americans adapted to their surroundings.

GETTING INTERESTED

1. Write the title of Part 1 on the chalkboard. Ask: The history of America begins with what journey? *(the journey of humans to North America)* Where do you think this journey will end? *(in the present-day United States)*

2. It has been said that America is not like a blanket—one piece of unbroken cloth of the same color. It is more like a quilt—of many pieces, of many colors. Ask students how the image of a quilt accurately describes the diversity of America. Call on volunteers to name some of the different groups who have settled in what is now the United States. Discuss how the movement of these peoples into the United States has produced the nation's diversity. Then ask: What is an American? At what time in history does the study of Americans begin? Who were the First Americans? Then tell students they will learn that the story of America begins in the Ice Age.

Working with Timelines
Remind students that a timeline shows events in chronological order. Have students construct a timeline on which they will record the important events or eras described in Part 1, from 40,000 B.C. to 10,000 B.C. (This can be an individual or a class activity.) Remind students that B.C. dates are counted "backward" from the year 1. Students should take notes as they read and make entries of dates after each appropriate chapter.

Using Maps
Have students turn to the world map on the back endpaper and then compare it with the map on page 15. Discuss how, over millions of years, the Earth's land masses shifted. How would these changes affect the movement of people? *(People who had been able to cross from one land mass to another were separated when water covered the land bridge.)*

History? Why?

In this chapter, Joy Hakim explains that no matter what their origins, all Americans have something in common: a history based upon a belief in democracy. While people of other nations share a common background, Americans are bound together by an idea: that government belongs to the people.

ASK

1. Why is history like a good mystery? *(No one knows the whole story of what happened in the past; new information turns up all the time.)*

2. Why is history especially important for Americans? *(Americans come from many different backgrounds; it's their shared history that ties them together.)*

3. What is the Constitution and what is unusual about who wrote it? *(It is the supreme law of our government, and was written by ordinary people who believed they could govern themselves.)*

4. How can the Constitution be changed? *(Amendments can be added to the Constitution.)*

 **Ponder**
Why did the author choose *A History of US* as her title rather than *A History of the U.S.?*

DISCUSS

1. The author says that the U.S. government isn't perfect and that "being fair to everyone in a large nation is very difficult." Do you agree? Explain. *(Governments are made up of people with human faults, which can explain, though not excuse, certain actions.)*

2. What responsibilities do Americans have to their government? *(to ask questions, think, and learn about issues in order to vote for government representatives)*

3. Why can the United States government rightly be called a "people's government?" *(The Declaration of Independence states that the government must have the support of the people; the Constitution was written by ordinary people and says that everyone, including members of the government, must obey the same laws.)*

✔ **Question Chart**

WRITE

Ask students to write a paragraph in response to this question: What is your opinion of the importance of history? Have them include a question they would like to have answered by reading *A History of US*.

L I T E R A C Y   L I N K S

Words to Discuss

democracy
Constitution
Declaration of Independence
amendments

Ask: How can you use these words to describe the U.S. government? *(The Declaration of Independence stated the goals of American independence; the Constitution is the law of America's government, which is a democracy of the people; amendments are laws that can change the Constitution.)*

Reading Skills
Identifying Perspective

Draw students' attention to the margin quotations on pages 8-11. Explain that the author of each quote expresses a different viewpoint, or perspective, on history. Post the following questions for partners to answer and share with the rest of the class. INFERRING

• Which authors have a humorous perspective? *(Henry Ford, Mark Twain)*

• Which authors talk about the importance of truth in writing about

history? *(Cicero and Miquel de Cervantes)*

• Why does Roger Wilkins believe strongly in the United States? *(It has tried to live up to the ideals set out by its founders; it has shown the ability to change.)*

• What do you think Marcus Garvey means by, "A man without history is like a tree without roots?" *(People have to feel connected to their past in order to thrive.)*

Away with Time

Who were the very first Americans? Although nobody knows for sure, many scientists believe the story began with the big-game hunters who inhabited northern Asia more than 40,000 years ago.

ASK

1. Where did the Stone Age people live? *(in Siberia, in northern Asia)*
2. What were some of the characteristics of the people from Siberia? *(They looked like modern East Asians and Native Americans; wore leather clothes; wove plant fibers into baskets and nets; made artwork; played a flute.)*
3. Why is the period of time about 40,000 years ago known as the Stone Age? *(People during this time made tools out of stone.)*
4. Why was the discovery of fire important to the early hunters? *(Fire allowed them to move north in search of game.)*

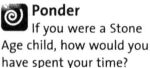 **Ponder**
If you were a Stone Age child, how would you have spent your time? What skills would you have had?

✔ **Question Chart**

DISCUSS

1. Why was making tools such an important step in the development of *Homo sapiens sapiens*? *(Tools allowed people to make things that were useful to them; tools made it possible for people to adapt better to their environment.)*
2. Why would tool-making have been so important to Stone Age humans? *(Tools helped them hunt large animals and make clothing and shelter and other objects.)*
3. Why do you think the author says that the hunters are on their way to America? *(They might follow the animals to new lands.)*

WRITE

Ask students to write a first-person narrative describing life for a Stone Age child. What might this child see or experience?

LITERACY LINKS

Words to Discuss

domesticated

Have students use a dictionary to determine the meaning of *domesticated*. Then have them look up the meaning of the root word *domestic*. Discuss: In what ways were Stone Age people domestic? *(They lived in homes and had families; they made things by hand.)*

Reading Skills
Using Timelines

Direct students' attention to the timeline on pages 12-13. What does the direction *Add four feet here* mean? Why doesn't the timeline show this period of time? *(This portion of the timeline represents 35,000 years; there is not enough space on the page to show that span of time.)* Ask students to subtract to find the date that would identify *Begin Farming*. *(5,000 B.C.)* ANALYZING

Skills Connection
Geography

Have students turn to the world map on pages 178-179 and help them identify the location of Siberia—in present-day Russia, north of Mongolia. Ask: What do you already know about the climate? *(very cold)* Lead students to understand that in the real world, this part of northeast Asia is very close to Alaska. If you have a globe, use it to demonstrate this to students.

In the Beginning

During the Ice Age, earth bridges between Asia and North America made it possible for people and animals to move into new regions. New evidence suggests that people may also have crossed the Pacific and Atlantic oceans by boat from Asia and Europe.

ASK

1. How might some of the first people have traveled to North America? *(by foot across the Beringia earth bridge; by sailing along the coast)* How long did this migration take? *(maybe a few thousand years)*

2. What was the land of Beringia like during the Ice Age? *(It was grassy, had lakes, and had a mild climate; it was 18 miles long and 1,000 miles wide.)*

3. What kinds of animals were in America? *(antelope, ox, sheep, lions, beaver, tigers, bison, etc.)*

4. Map: Have students use Resource 2 (TG page 73) to trace routes taken by the First Americans from Asia to North America.

◎ Ponder
Why are people now concerned about global warming and glaciers melting?

✓ Question Chart

DISCUSS

1. Why was North America a "hunter's heaven" at this time? *(It was full of huge animals.)*

2. What happened to the climate of North America about 10,000 years ago? How did that affect the movement of peoples to North America? *(The climate warmed up, melting the ice and covering Beringia with water. This stopped people from coming to or leaving North America.)*

3. The history of modern America includes waves of migration of people from the time of Columbus to the present. How is this similar to the migration of the First Americans? *(The First Americans did not all come at once; they came in different groups throughout the Ice Age, and found their way to different parts of the Americas.)*

WRITE

Ask students to write a short feature for their school newspaper titled "Living in Beringia." Ask them to describe the location and climate of Beringia, and the animals and people who lived there.

LITERACY LINKS

Words to Discuss

Ice Age
glacier
earth bridge
hunter-gatherers

Have students use context to define the words. Discuss: What term has the same meaning as *land bridge*? *(earth bridge)* What word describes a way of life? *(hunter-gatherers)*

Reading Skills
Using Text Features

Direct students to the margin note on page 14. Have them compare the estimated dates of the arrival of the First Americans *(15,000-30,000 years ago)* with the dates given in the feature Old Mysteries and New Discoveries on page 16 *(33,000 years ago, 22,000 years ago)*. Discuss: Why does this information appear in a margin note and in a feature? *(It gives extra facts that don't fit into the main body of the text.)* ANALYZING

Meeting Individual Needs
Visual Learners

Encourage students to use the map on page 15 to help explain the migration of people and animals from Asia to America. Read aloud the map's caption. Ask: How does the caption explain why we do not see Beringia on maps now? *(Beringia appeared when ocean levels were lower due to the glaciers. There are no glaciers now and ocean levels are higher.)*

How the First Americans Became Indians

After Beringia was submerged for the last time, contact between the Americas and the rest of the world was broken for about 10,000 years. During that time, the First Americans spread out in the Americas, adapted to their new surroundings, and developed diverse cultures.

ASK

Ponder
What do you think it must have been like to hunt large animals with Stone Age weapons?

Question Chart

1. How did the First Americans adjust to the disappearance of the large animals that they hunted for food? *(They hunted other animals, fished, gathered foods, and farmed.)*
2. What things did the First Americans develop or discover that we still use today? *(foods, plants and herbs that cure sickness, hammocks, canoes, snowshoes, lacrosse, rubber)*
3. The ancient Native Americans developed calendars, made rubber balls, and built pyramids. What invention did they not make? *(the wheel)*

DISCUSS

1. What are some reasons that the large Ice Age animals disappeared in North America? *(Huge animals didn't have enough water when the climate warmed up; excessive hunting; infection from human germs.)*
2. Why does the author say that the horse was returning home when the Spanish brought horses to America in the 1400s? *(An ancestor of the horse lived in America during the Ice Age; they had migrated to Asia and to Europe and grown bigger.)*

WRITE

Ask students to choose the invention or development made by the Native Americans that they think was most important and write a paragraph explaining their choice.

LITERACY LINKS

Words to Discuss

native
species
extinction

Have students use a dictionary to find which word includes the Latin word meaning "quench." *(extinct)*

Then ask them to write a sentence using all three words.

Reading Skills
Using Text Organization

Tell students that authors often organize nonfiction by stating a main idea and supporting it with details. Have partners find supporting details for each of the following main ideas. ANALYZING

- It makes sense to call the First Americans "Native Americans."
- The First Americans were good hunters.

Skills Connection
Geography

Have students look at the maps on pages 22, 23, and 178-179. Have them note the estimated dates of the earlier maps. Then ask them to describe what happened to North America over time. *(Over 200 million years ago, it was part of a large landmass that combined all of the continents; about 75 million years ago, it was split into several parts; today, it is one of seven continents.)*

THINKING ABOUT THE THEMES

The following questions will help students relate the book's themes to the content of Part 1. You may wish to use the questions for classroom discussion or have students answer them in written form.

1. Thousands of years ago, what was the most likely reason people moved from one place to another? *(to hunt animals and gather plants for food)*

2. What geographic conditions during the Ice Age made it possible for people to move into the Americas? *(lower sea levels; earth bridges connected Asia and America; smaller oceans made travel by boat easier)*

3. What accounts for the great diversity in the Americas? *(People came to America from many places, with different backgrounds, different skills, different languages.)*

4. Draw students' attention to the themes that have been posted around the room. Give them the opportunity to explore the relevance of these themes to Part 1. Accept choices that are supported by sound reasoning.

ASSESSING PART 1

Use Check-Up 1 (TG page 65) to assess student learning.

NOTE FROM JOY HAKIM

If I were teaching with A History US, I would begin by reading the first two chapters aloud with my students. Then I'd assign sizable portions of the book to be read on their own. It is not necessary for every student to understand every word. As long as they keep reading, they will be learning.

PROJECTS AND ACTIVITIES

▶ Designing a Book Cover

Ask students to imagine that all ten books of *A History of US* have been bound into a single volume that tells the story of America from the time of the Ice Age up to today. Have students design a cover illustrating a book that tells the whole story of the American people—showing all of the people who are US.

▶ Ice Age Animals

Have students draw a large Ice Age animal such as the mammoth, and then find out more about the animal in encyclopedias or another reference. They should use the information to write a caption for their drawing that includes facts about the animal, its size, its environment, and when it lived. Some students may wish to find out more about Ice Age animals by visiting the virtual exhibit *Mammoth Saga* at **www.mammsaga/welcome.html.en.**

▶ Archaeological Finds

Have students look at the pictures of the flint axes on pages 12 and 15 and remind them that archaeologists develop theories about long-ago people based partly on such items. Ask students to choose a modern tool, and then imagine that they are archaeologists 10,000 years in the future who have found this tool. How would they analyze this tool? What will the tool tell them about 21st-century Americans?

▶ Timeline

Have students compare their timelines to the Chronology of Events on pages 166-167. Have them read the What Is B.C.E? feature and then include these initials on their timelines.

★★ **FACTS TO SHARE** ★★

The scientist Spencer Wells believes that there were as few as two men, and at most a clan of 20 people, who were the first humans to migrate from Siberia to Alaska. Dr. Wells has written *The Journey of Man: A Genetic Odyssey*, in which he uses genetics to try to trace the movement of the first humans throughout the world. For more on *The Journey of Man*, go to **www.nationalgeographic.com**.

Adapting to a Diverse Land

For thousands of years, ancestors of today's Native Americans spread out over two continents. Part 2 leads student along some of the paths followed by Native Americans as they settled North America and adapted their lives to its varied geography. By 1492, they had developed ways of life as diverse as the North American landscape itself.

SETTING GOALS

The goals for students in Part 2 are to:
- understand how the Inuit and Native Americans adapted to and changed their environments.
- discover the varied social structures developed by Native Americans.
- chart the diversity of the First Americans.

GETTING INTERESTED

1. Native Americans eventually spread out from Alaska all the way to the tip of South America. In this migration, they encountered many environments. Ask: What are some different environments through which these peoples may have passed? *(cold, snowy; hot, dry deserts, woodlands, grasslands, tropical lands, and so on)* What changes might people have made in order to adapt to each of these environments? *(People would have changed their diet to adapt to the food supply; made shelters that were appropriate to their environments, using available materials; and worn clothing suitable to the climate.)*

2. In Part 2, Joy Hakim introduces several First American cultures from different regions at different points on the historical timeline. Ask students to skim the first paragraphs of Chapters 6, 7, 8, and 12 to understand the different time periods and regions the author discusses.

Working with Timelines
Remind students that we're certain that humans were living in the Americas by the year 10,500 B.C.E. Explain that Part 2 leaps ahead to look at North America in the centuries just before Columbus's arrival in 1492. Have students use the Chronology of Events on pages 166-167 to help them construct a timeline from 10,500 B.C. to 1400 that covers the time period in this Part.

Using Maps
Point out on a wall map of the United States the following regions: California coast, Pacific Northwest, Southwest, Great Plains, Southeast, Northeast, Alaska and Hawaii. Then assign small groups to study one of the regions shown on the front endpaper map. Ask: What do the map's illustrations tell you about each region and how people lived? Then have each group complete the following sentence: "We think that people in our region adapted to the environment by _____."

Put On Your Earmuffs

The frigid arctic and subarctic regions tested the ingenuity of the Inuit—the last wave of ancient Asian people to move into North America. These people, who have also been called Eskimos, arrived after Beringia had already been covered by water; they continue to live in the northern regions to this day.

ASK

. In what lands do the Inuit live? *(arctic and subarctic regions in Alaska, Canada, Greenland, and Siberia)*

. How did the Inuit travel to North America? Where had they come from? *(by sled over the polar ice; from northern Asia)*

. What is the climate like in the arctic region? *(It is below freezing for 10 months of the year and can be as cold as −50° F.)* How do you think the lack of sunlight affects the temperature in winter? *(It probably makes it colder because it is dark most of the day.)*

. **Map:** Have students begin to complete Resource 3 (TG page 74).

DISCUSS

. How did the Inuit adapt to their cold, harsh environment? *(eating raw fish and meat for vitamins, building igloos and pit houses, hunting, making warm clothing, developing kayaks and sleds, and so on)*

. Why do you think the Inuit stayed in the frigid north? *(The Inuit came from northern Asia; they were used to a fiercely cold climate and thrived in it; they may have been attacked when they headed south.)*

. What was different about the lives of the Inuit who lived on the coast and the Inuit who lived inland? *(People on the coast fished the seas and lived in pit houses; inland Inuit were nomads who hunted animals and cut holes through the ice to fish; many lived in igloos.)*

🌀 Ponder
If you were living in another region—a place where conditions are completely different from where you are now—how would you adapt?

✅ Question Chart

WRITE

The Inuit loved stories. Often, while telling a tale, a person would use an ivory "story nife" to draw pictures of the story in the snow. Have students write the beginning sentences of a made-up tale about Inuit life and then draw a picture to illustrate it.

L I T E R A C Y   L I N K S

Words to Discuss

Arctic	subarctic
tundra	taiga
nomad	

sk: Which word has the same meaning as *frozen desert*? *(tundra)* Which word means "treeless"? *taiga)* Have students check their esponses in a dictionary.

The prefix *sub-* means "below." How does this help describe the ocation of the *subarctic* region? *(The ubarctic must be the region below, or outh of, the Arctic.)*

Reading Skills
Comparing and Contrasting

Help students complete a two-column chart on the chalkboard contrasting the coastal Inuit and the nomadic inland Inuit. Students can compare hunting and fishing methods, housing, and the lands the people live on. SYNTHESIZING

Skills Connection
Geography

Direct students to the Arctic region on a classroom wall map. Discuss that, over thousands of years, the Inuit migrated from the eastern tip of Siberia across Alaska, northern Canada, and all the way to Greenland. Ask students to use the map scale to tell about how far the Inuit migrated. *(about 5,000 miles)*

Cliff Dwellers and Others

In the Four Corners region of the present-day Southwest, stone ruins perch along steep-sided cliffs. These silent monuments are reminders of the vanished Anasazi farmers, who probably are the ancestors of the Pueblo peoples of today.

ASK

1. Who are the descendants of the Anasazi, and where do they live? (*The Pueblo peoples; they live farther south near the Rio Grande.*) How do they keep some of the Anasazi culture alive? (*farm; live in adobe apartment-type houses*)

2. What is a kiva? What was it used for? (*A round room dug into the ground within the Anasazi cliffside village; men gathered there to make laws and hold religious ceremonies.*)

3. Where did the Anasazi farm? (*on flat land on the table mountain above the cliffs where they lived*)

4. What climate changes contributed to the end of the Anasazi community at Mesa Verde? (*a 24-year drought*)

5. **Map:** Have students mark the locations of the cultures mentioned in this chapter on Resource 3 (TG page 74).

Ponder
Is there a place in your community that is used by people in ways that are similar to how a kiva was used by the Anasazi?

✔ Question Chart

DISCUSS

1. What might be the advantages and disadvantages of living in stone apartments on the side of a cliff? (*Advantages: protection from snow and enemies; Disadvantages: damp, cramped apartments, difficult to get in and out*)

2. What activity was probably most important for the Anasazi? What details tell you this activity was important? (*farming; the growing of corn, the building of reservoirs, climbing to the cornfields every day, harvest festivals, most Anasazi men are farmers, leaving when farming is no longer possible*)

WRITE

Have students imagine that they live in an Anasazi village which has just enjoyed a successful corn harvest. Have them write invitations to the villagers announcing a festival to celebrate their good fortune. For ideas, students may reread the paragraph about such ceremonies on page 30.

LITERACY LINKS

Words to Discuss

kiva	council
Pueblo	mesa

Have students use context clues to define the words and then check their work in a dictionary. Ask: Which words relate to the Anasazi's community organization? (*kiva, council*) How are a mesa and a cliff related? (*A cliff is the steep side of a mesa.*)

Reading Skills
Identifying Point of View

Ask students to find phrases the author uses to describe the Anasazi community. (*a splendid home, a sharing community, and so on*) Ask: What do these phrases tell you about the author's opinion or feeling about the Anasazi? (*The author respects and admires the Anasazi and their accomplishments.*) INFERRING

Skills Connection
Geography

Have students locate the Four Corners region—where New Mexico, Arizona, Colorado, and Utah meet—on the map on page 184. Explain that Mesa Verde, where the Anasazi lived for about 800 years, is a tableland that stretches for 20 miles and is between 1,000 and 2,000 feet high.

The Show-Offs

The plentiful natural resources of the Pacific Northwest made life easy for its peoples. Their riches also encouraged class-oriented societies in which individual wealth brought prestige.

ASK

. How did the peoples of the Pacific Northwest get food? *(They fished for large sea animals, hunted game, and gathered berries, nuts, and roots.)* Why did the people have so much leisure time? *(Food and wood were easy to gather.)*

. What was important to these peoples? *(private property, wealth, and prestige)* What effect did this have on their society? *(People were not equals. The society was divided into classes based on wealth; people owned slaves.)*

. What is a potlatch? *(Potlatches were huge parties with much feasting. The party-giver gave away many possessions.)*

. **Map:** Have students continue to work on Resource 3 (TG page 74).

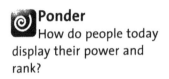**Ponder**
How do people today display their power and rank?

**Question Chart**

DISCUSS

. How was the structure of the society of the Northwest Coast people different from the society of the Anasazi? *(The Anasazi were a cooperative and communal group who lived close together and didn't have class differences. The Northwest Coast people amassed wealth for themselves and had different classes of people based on wealth.)*

. Do you think that a wood-carver might be well respected in a Northwest Coast society? *(Totem poles, masks, bowls, and houses all had wood carvings that were beautiful and showed off a family's wealth, so a wood-carver would probably be a valuable member of the society.)*

WRITE

Have students imagine they are European traders in the late 1700s who have been invited to a potlatch. Ask them to write a journal entry describing the potlatch. They should include details about the food that was served, the items that were given away, and how people entertained each other.

L I T E R A C Y   L I N K S

Words to Discuss

potlatch	totem
prestige	affluence

Have students make a synonym word web for each of the words. Have students compare their word webs and make additions to their own webs.

Reading Skills
Using Graphic Aids

Before reading the chapter, ask partners to preview the drawings and photographs and then answer the following questions. INFERRING

● What can you tell about the animal life of the Pacific Northwest? *(Frogs and fish seem important.)*

● What tools did people have? *(bows and arrows; canoes)*

● Did the people value beautiful objects? *(Yes, their artisans were skilled and made beautiful things.)*

Meeting Individual Needs
Reteaching

If students have difficulty pronouncing Native American names, have the class create a Native American dictionary with pronunciations and definitions for each word.

Taking a Tour

A sweeping panorama of North America reveals the geographic and cultural patterns in the 1400s. It becomes clear that there was no such thing as a "typical" Native American culture and that geography played an important part in determining the culture and customs of native peoples.

ASK

1. What evidence supports the author's statement that there was no such thing as a "typical" Native American people? *(Native Americans spoke 250 languages and lived in and adapted to many different environments.)*

2. What is the largest river in North America? What are its two largest branches? *(Mississippi River; Missouri River and Ohio River)*

3. What is the main feature of the land between the Mississippi River and the Atlantic Ocean? *(forests)*

 Ponder
How would a spin over the continent today be different from one in the 15th century?

 Question Chart

DISCUSS

1. What does the author mean by saying that the Mississippi River splits the land in two—but not in half? *(The river runs from north to south, dividing the land, but the land west of the river is twice as large as the land east of the river.)*

2. In the 1400s, why do you suppose California was one of the most densely populated regions of the continent? *(There was an abundance of food and a mild climate, and most of the tribes lived peacefully with each other.)*

3. Think about this chapter's title, "Taking a Tour." What does this tour help you to understand? *(what the main features of the land in the U.S. looked like in the 1400s; that native peoples who lived in each region must have lived differently, according to the climate and the natural resources that were available)*

WRITE

Have partners write a dialogue featuring a time capsule tour guide and a passenger. The tour guide should be directing the passenger to look at various sights mentioned in this chapter, and the passenger can make comments and ask questions about the sights.

LITERACY LINKS

Words to Discuss

tribe   sierra
people

Discuss: Which two words describe groupings of Native Americans? *(tribe, people)* Why would it be difficult to cross a sierra? *(It is a long, jagged mountain chain.)*

Reading Skills
Evaluating Rhetorical Devices

Ask: What do you think are the author's purposes in having readers imagine that they are in a time capsule with her? *(to keep readers aware of time and place, to put readers "in the picture")* How does it help you visualize how the continent looked in the past? CONNECTING

Meeting Individual Needs
Visual/Spatial Learners

Visual and spatial learners will benefit from following the west-to-east journey described in this chapter on a wall map of the United States or on the map on pages 182-183. Make sure students begin in the west as they trace the journey.

Plains Indians Are Not Plain At All

By the year 1000, the disappearance of the big game forced hunters on the central plains to adapt to the harsh prairie environment. They hunted buffalo on foot until the 16th century, when the Spaniards introduced horses.

ASK

. What are some of the features of the Plains? *(windy, dry, extremes of hot and cold, few forests, flat land, tall grasses)*

. Why were the Plains Indians nomads who followed the buffalo? *(Farming was difficult, and the buffalo provided food and materials for shelter, clothing, and tools.)*

. When did the Spaniards explore the plains? *(in the 16th century)*

. **Map:** Have students continue to work on Resource 3 (TG page 74).

DISCUSS

.. How did contact with Europeans change the lives of the Plains Indians? *(Trading for horses and metal knives gave Plains Indians the freedom to move long distances rapidly and made them better hunters, warriors, and traders. They gained wealth and power.)*

.. Why did the buffalo almost become extinct in the 19th century? *(The Plains people now had guns as well as horses, making it even easier to hunt buffalo; they hunted buffalo in bigger numbers; others hunted them wastefully. Have students speculate who the others will be.)*

.. Direct students to the How Did They Say "Mom"? feature on page 46. Ask: How does the study of language help historians learn about ancient peoples? *(It helps them trace a people's origins through common language groups.)*

◎ Ponder
What do you think it was like to hunt buffalo on foot? What qualities would a person need to do this?

☑ Question Chart

WRITE

Ask students to write a paragraph comparing and contrasting the lives of Plains people before and after contact with Europeans.

LITERACY LINKS

Words to Discuss

prairie   tepee

Have students look up these words in dictionary. Ask: Why was a tepee a good shelter for nomadic people? *(It was easy to put up, take down, and move.)* Why did the Indians move around the prairie? *(to follow the buffalo)*

Reading Skills
Understanding Primary and Secondary Sources

Point out the primary source quotation in italics on page 43. Elicit who wrote these words. *(a Spaniard traveling with Coronado)* Ask: Did this person witness the events he writes about? *(yes)* Why would the author use this eyewitness description instead of her own words to tell how the people used the buffalo? *(A firsthand description adds interest, supports the author's argument, makes the description seem more "true," and helps readers feel that they are part of the scene.)* SYNTHESIZING

Meeting Individual Needs
English Language Learners

For the benefit of students learning English, read aloud the text of the primary source journal on page 43. Then read it again, inviting students to help you paraphrase each sentence. Explain unfamiliar words, including the definitions in the margin of *sinew*, *awls*, and *dung*.

Mound for Mound, Those Are Heavy Hills

For more than 2,000 years, the Mound Builders marked their presence with earthen structures that rivaled the pyramids. The last of these cultures, the Mississippians, thrived around 300 B.C.E. Eventually, like the Anasazi, the Mound Builders disappeared mysteriously.

ASK

 Ponder
Why did the Mound Builders make such amazing mounds? Was someone or something meant to see them?

 Question Chart

1. Where did the Mound Builders live? Why might these people have built mounds? *(between the Mississippi and the Appalachians; for graves, platforms for temples and palaces or other religious reasons, government centers, defense against enemies)*

2. What did archaeologists discover at the Hopewell Mound? What did these objects tell them about the Hopewell civilization? *(They found objects from far away such as sharks' teeth, shells, obsidian, and copper; it showed that they were traders and had a sophisticated culture at the same time that Jesus lived.)*

3. What was Cahokia? What was the social structure in Cahokia? *(the large center of the Mississippians; it was a slave society with a ruler, nobles, and "stinkards" or slaves.)*

4. **Map:** Have students add information about the Mound Builders on Resource 3 (TG page 74).

DISCUSS

1. What are some ideas about why the mound-building cultures disappeared? *(overpopulation, not enough resources, poor sanitation and sickness, enemy attack, or rejection of slavery)*

2. Does the text give facts or opinions about the purpose for which the Mound Builders created earthen designs? Why? *(opinions, because the reasons are unknown)*

3. Have students complete Resource 4 (TG pages 75-76). Making an outline will help them organize information about the Adena, Hopewell, and Mississipian cultures.

WRITE

Ask students to choose a mound and describe it for a young people's travel guide of America. They should include historical information and details from the text. Students may want to make a drawing to illustrate their descriptions.

L I T E R A C Y   L I N K S

Words to Discuss

artifact   **archaeologist**

Have students find definitions for these words in a dictionary. Ask: Why are ancient artifacts so important to archaeologists? *(They provide clues to cultures of the past.)* What artifacts does our culture produce that might provide clues to archaeologists of the future?

Reading Skills
Distinguishing Between Fact and Opinion

Help students find words on page 50 that signal opinions. *(Maybe; Some experts think; Perhaps)* Discuss: When the author uses words like *maybe* and *perhaps*, what does she want you to know? *(She is telling you what she thinks; she is giving an opinion that cannot be proven.)* Have students write several statements of fact and opinion about the Mound Builders. ANALYZING

Skills Connection
Math

Help students draw a scale model of the 1,300-foot-long Snake Mound. Suggest that they use the scale 1" = 50' and cut a piece of string to that length (26 inches). They can use the string and a large piece of paper to help them draw the Snake Mound. Ask: What details in the text will help you draw the snake? *(a huge curving snake, its mouth is open and it is swallowing something)*

Indians of the Eastern Forests

In the Eastern Woodlands, native peoples practiced hunting and gathering, fishing, and slash-and-burn farming. Most of the people were Algonquins. Their major enemy was the Iroquois.

ASK

1. How did the Woodland Indians adapt to life in the forests? *(They hunted game, girdled trees to make clearings, lived in wigwams made from trees and vines, and developed slash-and-burn farming.)*

2. How were the tribes of the Algonquian peoples related? *(by the languages they spoke and their common customs; through trade and friendship)*

3. Who gave the Iroquois people their name? What does the name mean? *(the Algonquins; in Algonquian, Iroquois means "terrible people")*

4. **Map:** Have students add the Eastern Woodland Indians to Resource 3 (TG page 74).

DISCUSS

1. What is slash-and-burn farming? Why was this a good farming method in the eastern forests? *(The method of clearing trees, burning branches and fertilizing the earth with ashes, cultivating the soil and then planting; the area was full of trees which had to be cleared away in order to have a place to plant; it was a way of enriching the soil.)*

2. Today, the eastern United States could be described as having flat land, cities, highways, and skyscrapers. How would you describe the appearance of the eastern region when it was inhabited by the Woodland Indians? *(The region was covered by huge, ancient forests which provided materials for building and hunting and shelter for animals; it was dotted with Indian villages.)*

3. How did Eastern Woodlands people decorate themselves? *(With makeup, jewelry, and hair styles; people had tattoos and hunters blackened their teeth with ash.)*

◎ Ponder
What do you think it was like to live in a longhouse with 20 families? How did everybody manage to get along?

 **Question Chart**

WRITE

Have students suppose they are Europeans in the 1500s. Have them write a letter to a friend in their home country about an encounter with some Algonquian people.

L I T E R A C Y   L I N K S

Words to Discuss

slash-and-burn   cultivate
diligently

The text says that the Indians "till the soil very *diligently*." Ask: Do you think this made them successful farmers? Why? What do you do *diligently*?

Reading Skills
Evaluating Illustrations

Draw students' attention to the picture by Jacques LeMoyne on page 53. What activity does the picture show? *(planting and cultivating the soil)* How would you describe the heads of the women? *(fair skinned; long, curly hair that looks light in color; European looking)* Why do you think LeMoyne drew the Indians this way? *(He may have wanted to represent people in a way that was familiar to Europeans.)* VISUALIZING

Skills Connection
Geography

Have students refer to the Resources map on pages 182-183 to find out more about the resources available to Eastern Woodland Indians. Then have them identify resources available to the other Native American cultures they have read about.

People of the Long House

To end warfare amongst themselves, the Iroquois formed a democratic confederacy that united five nations. (Later, a sixth nation joined.) Each nation made laws for itself, but important matters were discussed jointly at the yearly Great Council. This remarkable plan of government astounded and inspired Europeans.

ASK

1. How was the Iroquois confederacy organized? *(Each nation had its own identity and laws. In matters of war or common concerns, a council of sachems from each nation made unanimous decisions.)*
2. What convinced Deganwidah and Hiawatha that the Iroquois council should be formed? *(They were tired of wars of revenge and wanted peace among the five nations.)*
3. Why was the ability to speak eloquently or to persuade others valued at the council? *(Decisions had to be unanimous; so people who convinced others were important.)*
4. What did the Europeans think about the Indians? What was fundamentally wrong about their view? *(Europeans thought the Indians were savages; the Indians had civilizations, with governments, religious beliefs, and cultural achievements.)*
5. **Map:** Have students complete Resource 3 (TG page 74).

 Ponder

What items, apart from books or letters, would help tell your family or community's history, as wampum did for the Indians?

✔ **Question Chart**

DISCUSS

1. How did women influence the Iroquois council? Why did they have such influence? *(The women chose the sachems who represented each nation. The women were the leaders of the clans; they were respected for their skill at farming.)*
2. What might be difficult about a government that must make unanimous decisions, as the Iroquois council did? *(It may take a long time for everyone to agree on a decision; some people might feel forced into going along with the majority decision.)*

WRITE

Hiawatha wanted to convert the tyrant Tadodaho to ways of peace. Have students write a speech for Hiawatha in which he tries to persuade Tadodaho to change his ways.

LITERACY LINKS

Words to Discuss

sachem   confederacy
unanimous   oratory
Iroquois League

Have students use a dictionary.
- Which word comes from the Latin for "one mind"? *(unanimous)*
- Which means "someone making a speech": *orator* or *oratory*? *(orator)*
- Which word means "a league" or "an alliance of nations"? *(confederacy)*

Reading Skills
Analyzing Word Choice

Explain that both the Native Americans and the Europeans came to view each other as uncivilized. "Uncivilized" is a loaded word—it suggests a strong, negative meaning. Elicit that sometimes one group calls another group "uncivilized" because they are different or because they are ignorant of the other group's culture. Discuss: How can cultural differences lead to misunderstanding?
CONNECTING

Skills Connection
History/Literature

Point out that historians are not the only people who write about history; novelists, poets, and songwriters do, too. Direct students to the margin note about Longfellow's "Hiawatha" on page 59. Interested students may want to begin a bibliography of historical fiction, poems, and songs that they read about in *The First Americans*. They might use the bibliography to do independent reading.

THINKING ABOUT THE THEMES

The following questions will help students relate the book's themes to the content of Part 2. You may wish to use the questions for classroom discussion or have students answer them in written form.

How did varied environments lead to diverse ways of life among Native Americans? *(The Native Americans were completely dependent on the natural world for everything they built, made, and ate, and the activities they pursued. So, differences in the ways in which they adapted to their environments led to differences in their ways of life.)*

Give examples of how the diversity of the Native American cultures was reflected in their structures of their societies. *(The Northwest Indians and Mississippians kept slaves; the Anasazi worked together and had a council; the Iroquois nations formed a confederacy.)*

Draw students' attention to the other themes that have been posted around the room. Give them the opportunity to explore the relevance of these themes to Part 2. Accept choices that are supported by sound reasoning.

ASSESSING PART 2

Use Check-Up 2 (TG page 66) to assess student learning.

NOTE FROM JOY HAKIM

I like timelines. In trying to convey the concept of time, I often take a ruler and a long string into the classroom. I hold up the ruler and ask the children to imagine that it represents 1,000 years of time. Then we measure off 40 lengths of ruler on the string. (Some experts guess that is about when the first peoples stepped onto the American continent.) Then I ask the children when Columbus arrived. I take a red marker and mark the answer to that question—half a ruler length—on the string. The contrast makes a big impression.

PROJECTS AND ACTIVITIES

▶ Native American Cultures Chart

Distribute Resource 5 (TG page 77). Have students fill out the chart with information about the Native American cultures discussed in Part 2.

▶ Relating Past and Present

Point out to students that today's Native American peoples are descendants of the First Americans and that they will be studying Native American peoples at many points in *A History of US*. Encourage Native American students in your class or school to share descriptions of their cultural life with the class.

▶ Early American Architecture

Have students skim Part 2 to find examples of the different kinds of houses built by Native Americans. Have groups of students represent each structure by making drawings, paintings, or clay or craft stick models of each kind of structure. Groups can then create an exhibit of their work to present to the class.

▶ Songs to Celebrate

Tell students that most Native American peoples wrote songs that celebrated the success of a hunt, the harvesting of a crop, or the continued bounty of nature. Declared one Hopi song:

> Corn-blossom maidens
> Here in the fields,
> Patches of beans in flower,
> Fields all abloom, . . .
> Now behold!

Have students write lyrics of a song about an animal, a crop, or a plant important to one of the Native American peoples.

Expanding European Horizons

Part 3 highlights milestones in the journeys of the Europeans to the Americas. In the Age of Exploration in the 1400s, Europeans discovered oceans and continents that had been unknown to them. At the same time, the people from two different worlds were forced to adapt their thinking about the earth, themselves, and the future.

SETTING GOALS

The goals for students in Part 3 are to:

- describe the journeys and discoveries of the Vikings, Columbus, Balboa, Magellan, and Vespucci.
- learn about the advances in technology, science, and world view that led to Europe's Age of Discovery.
- understand the interactions between Native Americans and Europeans.

GETTING INTERESTED

1. Write the title of Part 3 on the chalkboard. Discuss that *horizon* can mean the line where the sky seems to meet the ocean, or the limit of a person's experience or understanding. Why might both meanings of the word work when discussing the European Age of Exploration? *(The explorers will probably go to sea; they will learn new things)*

2. Ask students to look at the navigation instruments on page 66. What do these instruments do? *(help sailors find their way on the seas)* How would they feel about setting out to sea with such instruments? Have students discuss how they think people today navigate. *(computers, radar)*

Working with Timelines

Elicit why 1492 is an important date in world history. *(It is the year Columbus crossed the Atlantic and reached the Americas.)* Ask: In what century is 1492? *(15th century)* With students, preview the author's discussion of centuries on page 67. Then ask them to find the date 1492 in the Chronology of Events on page 167.

Interpreting Maps

Have students preview the maps in Part 3. Ask volunteers to discuss what part of the world each map shows. Then have students turn to the map on pages 94-95 and note that it looks "wrong." Discuss that old maps like these can tell us what people knew about the physical world long ago. What did people who lived at this time—1507—know, or not know, about our world?

Let's Turn North

Most historians believe that the Vikings charted the first ocean routes to North America, although the extent of their explorations still remains a mystery. New research in archaeology, literature, anthropology, and zoology may yet answer questions about the range of Viking exploration and settlements.

ASK

1. What are some reasons the Vikings went exploring? *(overcrowded homelands, desire for loot, search for good land and fishing)*
2. Where is Vinland? *(in Newfoundland, in present-day Canada)*
3. Direct students to the picture of the Viking ship on page 63. Ask: How could the Vikings travel so far over the ocean in these boats? *(They were brave people; they were good sailors.)*
4. What fields of study help historians find out what happened in the past? *(archaeology, literature, anthropology, zoology)*
5. How do we know that Vikings settled in Newfoundland around the year 1000? *(from radiocarbon dating, stories in ancient literature, similarities to Viking houses, zoological clues, old maps)*

◎ Ponder
What fears would early sailors have to face when sailing far out into the ocean, out of sight of land?

 **Question Chart**

DISCUSS

1. What is the evidence that leads people to think that Vikings had arrived in North America? *(a spindle and the remains of Viking-style longhouses found in Newfoundland; a sea snail native to Scandinavia found in America; a map of a place called "Vinland," saying that it was "discovered" by Bjarni and Leif—two known Norse sailors)*
2. Direct students to the Atlas, pages 180-181. Ask: If the Vikings did reach Minnesota by water, how could they have done it? *(by traveling up the St. Lawrence River and sailing through the Great Lakes to Minnesota)*
3. Why don't experts always agree on what ancient artifacts and evidence say about the Norsemen? *(New evidence keeps turning up, people raise new questions.)*

WRITE

The year is about 987. Leif Eriksson is planning a sea voyage from Scandinavia. He needs people to accompany him on his ship. Write a newspaper advertisement that he could have composed, trying to convince sailors to come along.

L I T E R A C Y   L I N K S

Words to Discuss

anthropology   zoology

Have students use a dictionary to find the meaning of the suffix -*ology*. *("a subject of study")* and to find the word parts and definitions of *anthropology* and *zoology*. Ask: How does knowing the meaning of the suffix help you determine the meaning of a word like *climatology*?

Reading Skills
Using Photographs

Direct students to the Vikings at L'Anse aux Meadows feature on page 64. Ask: How does seeing this recreation of a Viking settlement help you form a mental picture of how the Vikings lived? Does it seem as if you would be comfortable there? *(Responses will vary.)* CONNECTING

Skills Connection
Geography

Have students look at the map on page 61. Discuss that the map shows features of the land in Scandinavia, Vinland, and Greenland. Ask: What land features are shown? *(Vinland and Scandinavia are hilly, Greenland is covered with ice)* Tell students that physical maps show land features such as mountains, plains, and plateaus.

The Power of the Press

One of the key events in the history of Europe was the invention of the printing press in 1454. During the 15th century new art, ideas, and inventions inspired Europeans to look beyond their own narrow horizons. For Prince Henry of Portugal, as well as other Europeans, that meant finding a sea route to the Indies.

ASK

1. What was Johannes Gutenberg's accomplishment in 1454? *(He was the first European to print a book—the Bible—with a printing press that used movable type.)*
2. Why was this so important? *(Before Gutenberg, almost all Europeans had no access to books or learning, and few people could read.)*
3. Why was Prince Henry of Portugal so important? *(He was a ruler who was interested in exploration; he attracted scientists, mapmakers, and sailors to Lisbon; he encouraged the effort to find a water route around Africa to the Indies and China.)*
4. Why did Europeans head out across unknown seas? *(They wanted power, and desired knowledge, fame and fortune. Marco Polo's book inspired them to reach the Indies, and overland travel to the Indies was dangerous.)*

🌀 Ponder
What do you think it was like living before the Internet? before computers? before books and newspapers?

✔ Question Chart

DISCUSS

1. Which invention do you think was more important to Europe—the compass or the printing press? *(Discussion should bring out that both inventions had far-reaching effects on Europe.)*
2. Why does the author call the 15th century the first Information Age? *(The printing press encouraged the growth of literacy and helped spread knowledge.)*
3. Do you think that sailors and navigators were more willing to undertake explorations after the improvement in the compass? *(Yes; although they had been able to navigate by the stars and had astrolabes, the magnetic compass was a better, more reliable tool.)*

WRITE

Have students write a brief essay about Henry the Navigator, describing his achievements and his personality. Ask them to include a prediction about what Henry might be doing today, and where he might be working.

LITERACY LINKS

Words to Discuss

Renaissance	navigator
scribe	movable type
compass	Indies

Have students use context to determine the meanings. Ask: Which word names a time period in the 15th century? *(Renaissance)* Which word is a name for East Asia? *(Indies)* Which two words name professions? *(navigator, scribe)* inventions? *(movable type, compass)*

Reading Skills
Identifying Cause and Effect

Have students complete a two-column chart on the chalkboard headed *Cause* and *Effect*. Under *Cause*, write *printing press invented*; ask students to name an effect. *(books available to more people)* Then have students find and list other causes and effects in the chapter, reminding them that a cause may have more than one effect. CONNECTING

Skills Connection
Geography

Have students use the world map on pages 178-179 and the inset map of Europe to locate Portugal. Then ask them to locate China and trace a possible sea route that Prince Henry had in mind around Africa to China. Ask: What ocean lies between Africa and Asia? *(Indian Ocean)* What islands would navigators have had to find their way around to sail from Africa to China? *(Indonesia, Malaysia, Philippines)*

A Boy Named Christopher Has a Dream

As a boy, Christopher Columbus dreamed of sailing to China. Columbus later became a skilled navigator, but his plan of sailing west to get to the Indies had one flaw—the earth is much larger than he thought.

ASK

. What is the difference between latitude and longitude? *(Latitude measures distance north and south of the equator. Longitude measures distance (and time) east and west of the prime meridian.)*

. What geographic facts did Columbus have correct? *(The world is round, Spain and Japan are at the same latitude.)* Which facts did he have wrong? *(Continents block the route west to Japan; the earth's size.)*

. What did the early explorers use to tell time? *(an hourglass)* How does knowing the time it takes to go from one point to another help sailors navigate? *(Knowing how much time passed lets you measure longitude; without knowing the longitude, sailors didn't know their exact location.)*

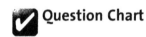**Ponder**
What would inspire you to begin a journey or decide on a field of study, as Marco Polo's book did for Columbus?

✔ **Question Chart**

DISCUSS

. Portuguese mathematicians figured the earth was much larger than Columbus thought. Why do you think Columbus still believed he could sail a western route to the Indies? *(No one had sailed around the globe so no one could be sure of its size; Columbus may have thought he could get to the Indies no matter how far away they were.)*

. What are the most important differences between the actual world and the German map on page 73? *(On the map on page 73, the oceans are much larger, North and South America are missing, the shapes of the continents are not correct.)*

WRITE

Have students write a letter from Columbus to King Ferdinand and Queen Isabel trying to persuade them to support his exploration. They should give details Columbus would have included to convince the Spanish leaders that he would succeed.

L I T E R A C Y   L I N K S

Words to Discuss

longitude	parallels
latitude	meridians
hemisphere	

Have students use context to discuss the words. Then have them refer to the globe on page 71 and use the vocabulary to identify and discuss each of the lines shown on the globe. Tell students that hemisphere comes from the Greek: *hemi* means "half"; *phere* means "ball."

Reading Skills
Analyzing Text Features

Direct students to the margin note on page 72 and the caption on page 73. Post these questions for partners to answer. SYNTHESIZING

• How were Eratosthenes and Ptolemy alike? *(Both were Greeks, lived in Egypt, and were mathematicians and geographers.)*

• Whose map did Columbus use? How old was it? *(Ptolemy's; 1,300 years)*

Skills Connection
Geography/Mathematics

Using a map of the world, have students determine to the nearest 5 degrees the latitude and longitude of the place where you live. Ask: Between what lines of latitude does most of the continental U.S. lie? *(30°N and 50°N)* Between what meridians of longitude? *(70°W and 120°W)*

A New Land Is "Discovered"

Christopher Columbus staked his life and reputation on a fear-filled journey across the Atlantic Ocean. Finally, on October 12, 1492, Europeans and Native Americans first encountered each other on San Salvador, an island in the Caribbean.

ASK

1. Where did Columbus intend to go on his journey? *(Cathay or China)* Where did he actually land? *(San Salvador, or Hispaniola, in the Caribbean islands)*
2. What problems did Columbus face on his first voyage? *(unreliable compass, Sargasso Sea, length of the journey, rough seas, threatened mutiny)*
3. How did the Taino treat Columbus and his men? *(They were friendly and generous, they took him to Cuba to help him find gold.)*

Ponder
If you were a member of Columbus's crew or one of the Taino, what would your impressions of the new people have been? Would you have been fearful? curious? puzzled?

Question Chart

DISCUSS

1. In what ways would you say Columbus's journey was a success? *(He sailed across the Atlantic Ocean and reached land near North America. He made contact with previously unknown people. He found pearls and gold.)*
2. In what ways might Columbus's journey be considered a failure? *(Columbus did not reach Cathay and never would. Innocent Taino people were harmed or enslaved. He would never find the riches he was expecting.)*
3. What was Columbus's attitude toward the Taino? *(Columbus said they were friendly and wrote about them in a complimentary way. He also took some as slaves and believed he had the right to do with them as he pleased.)*
4. Have students complete Resource 5 (TG page 78).

WRITE

A young sailor knows of Columbus's reputation and his goal. Eager to join his crew, the sailor writes to Columbus. Have students compose this letter.

LITERACY LINKS

Words to Discuss

immunity   **mutiny**

Have students use a dictionary and context to determine the meaning of the words. Tell them that vaccinations have given them *immunity* to several diseases. Ask: Do you know which diseases you have immunity to? *(small pox, diptheria, chicken pox)* Tell students that *Mutiny on the Bounty* is the name of a book (and movie) about sailors that take command of a ship from their cruel captain.

Reading Skills
Evaluating Author's Purpose

Explain that historians analyze primary sources to determine their purpose and to check for bias toward a certain point of view. Have students reread Columbus's letter on page 79. Help students evaluate the letter with the following questions. ANALYZING

- What purposes might Columbus have had in writing this letter? *(to report his discoveries; to make his trip seem successful)*
- What might he have wanted from Spain's treasurer? *(more money)*

- What was Columbus's purpose in writing this letter? *(He was probably trying to be positive; he needed to convince the treasurer that his voyage was a success.)*

Meeting Individual Needs
English Language Learners

Ask students to use the arrows on the map on page 77 to describe Columbus's route from Spain to San Salvador and back to Spain. Ask: How many ships returned to Spain? *(two)* How many started out? *(three)* Did the ships follow the same route on their return trip? *(No, they sailed a more northerly route.)*

The Next Voyage

Columbus's second voyage turned up neither gold nor a route to China. However, as Columbus continued to travel the Atlantic, a quiet revolution trailed in the wake of his ships. It is known today as the Columbian Exchange.

ASK

1. Why did the first Spanish settlement in Hispaniola fail? *(Settlers battled among themselves; Native Americans rebelled at their mistreatment and killed settlers.)*

2. What was the Columbian Exchange? *(the movement of plants and animals between the Old World and the New World and soon between four continents.)*

3. What lands did Columbus discover during his voyages? *(islands in the Caribbean but not the mainland of North America; South America, although he didn't think it was a continent)*

4. What were Columbus's reasons for thinking South America was the Garden of Eden? *(South America was lush, with a lot of birds and flowers; it reminded him of the place the Bible describes.)*

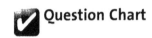**Ponder**
Which foods that you eat came from the Old World? Which originated in the New World?

Question Chart

DISCUSS

1. Do you think Columbus would have had much trouble raising money in Spain for a second trip to the so-called Indies? for a third trip? *(No, because he had brought back treasures and promised more; he was given many more ships. Yes, because he had again failed to find China or gold mines.)*

2. What became of the Indians on the islands after Columbus's second voyage? *(They were captured and used or sold as slaves; many died.)*

3. What do you predict Europeans' reaction would be when they learned that there was a continent that they hadn't known about ? *(They would want to explore it; they would be interested in what existed there, what would be useful to them.)*

WRITE

Have students reread the margin note on the Columbian Exchange on page 82, and then write a dialogue between a person from the Old World and one from the New World concerning the items that each world is giving to the other.

LITERACY LINKS

Words to Discuss

revolution
Columbian Exchange
barbarian

Have students use a dictionary and context to determine the meaning of the words. Ask: Why does the author say that Columbus helped start an agricultural "revolution"? *(Because of the Columbus Exchange, there was a great change in the crops grown by American and European farmers.)*

Reading Skills
Identifying Cause and Effect

Point out that a chain of events occurs when a cause triggers an effect, which triggers another effect, and so on. On the chalkboard, have students complete the causal chain that led to the beginning of slavery in America. Begin by writing *Cause: The Spanish brought disease to the Taino. (Effect: The Taino began to die. Effect: The Spaniards lacked workers. Effect: They enslaved Africans and brought them to the islands.)* SYNTHESIZING

Skills Connection
Charts and Graphs

Have students chart the plants and animals that were part of the Columbian Exchange by completing Resource 7 (TG page 79).

Stowaways: Worms and a Dog

On his fourth voyage, Columbus was marooned in Jamaica for a year. When he returned to Spain, he was largely ignored, although his voyages inspired other explorers, including Cabot, Balboa, and Pizarro.

ASK

1. What did worms have to do with Columbus's fourth voyage? *(Worms ate holes in the ships and Columbus was marooned in Jamaica and had to be rescued.)*
2. How did the Italian Giovanni Caboto (John Cabot) pave the way for England's claims to North America? *(England backed Cabot's voyage; Cabot landed in Newfoundland in North America.)*
3. What were Balboa's main accomplishments? *(He founded the first permanent European settlement in the Americas; he was the first European to see the Pacific Ocean from America.)*
4. What prompted Balboa to journey across Panama? *(to find the gold that Comaco had told him about; to see the ocean that Comaco talked about; to explore)*

 Ponder
Have you ever been very interested in something that other people don't care much about? What things do other people care about that don't interest you at all?

 Question Chart

DISCUSS

1. How did Columbus trick the people of Jamaica into feeding his men? *(His astronomical charts predicted an eclipse of the moon; Columbus told the chiefs if they didn't feed them he would blot out the moon; when the eclipse passed, they were fed.)*
2. What do you think were the effects on Europeans of Columbus's "discovery" of the Americas and Balboa's "discovery" of the Pacific Ocean? *(They became curious; they longed for further explorations; they were full of wonder and confusion about the new lands and the Pacific Ocean.)*

WRITE

Have students write a paragraph describing the highlights of Balboa's journey from Hispaniola to the Pacific Ocean and his march across Panama and back. They should include a description of the difficulty of exploring a foreign land.

LITERACY LINKS

Words to Discuss

marooned   conquistador
stowaway   eclipse
treason

Have students use context to define the words. Ask: Which two words might a sailor use? *(marooned, stowaway)* Which word would an astronomer use? *(eclipse)* Which two words might be used by a European soldier in the 1500s? *(treason, conquistador)*

Reading Skills
Drawing Conclusions

Have students use information in the text and the following questions to draw conclusions about Comaco and Balboa. INFERRING

- Why did Comaco tell Balboa where to find gold? *(His daughter had married Balboa; he was willing to help him.)*
- What did Comaco value more: gold or peace of mind? *(peace of mind)*
- How would you describe Balboa's personality? *(courageous, determined, inventive)*

Skills Connection
Geography

Have students locate Darien (Panama) on the map on pages 178-179. Ask students to discuss why the Panama Canal is now such an important trade route. *(It allows passage from the Atlantic Ocean to the Pacific Ocean, without having to go around South America.)*

Sailing Around the World

This chapter describes an expedition started by Ferdinand Magellan, which completed the first European journey around the globe. This voyage revealed the true size—and diversity—of our world.

ASK

. Where is the Strait of Magellan? *(between the southern tip of South America and Tierra del Fuego)* Why did it take Magellan so long to sail through it? *(The passageway is treacherous; it is stormy and has steep, rocky sides.)*

. How do historians know about Magellan's journey? *(by reading the journal kept by the Italian crew member Pigafetta.)*

. When did Magellan realize he had crossed the Pacific Ocean? *(when the slave Enrique spoke to people in the Philippines and they understood him)* How long did it take one of his ships to complete this round-the-world journey? *(almost three years)*

DISCUSS

. What are some details that support Pigafetta's view that Magellan "was more constant . . . than ever was any other." *(Magellan never gave up in the face of difficulty; he stood by the King of Cebu, although it cost him his life.)*

. What was the main significance of Magellan's voyage? *(It was the first expedition to circle the globe; the journey showed the true size of the earth.)*

. How would you compare Magellan and Balboa's relations with native peoples with Columbus's relations? *(Magellan and Balboa got along with the native peoples and seemed to respect and even admire them; Columbus fought with them and didn't seem to respect them.)*

WRITE

Magellan's voyagers have returned to Spain. A newspaper reporter wants to write an article about the journey. Have student pairs—one as the reporter and the other as the sailor—write up interviews.

⊚**Ponder**
Magellan and his men ate some pretty disgusting things to stay alive. Can you imagine yourself doing the same?

 **Question Chart**

LITERACY LINKS

Words to Discuss

strait

Ask students to look up *strait* in the dictionary. Then have them turn to the map on pages 178-179 and locate other passageways that might be straits. Tell students that a homophone is a word that has the same sound as another word but differs in spelling and meaning. Ask: What is a homophone for strait? *(straight: continuing in the same direction without curving).*

Reading Skills
Identifying Primary and Secondary Sources

Elicit from students that the italicized passages in the chapter are from Pigafetta's journal—a primary source. Ask: When did Pigafetta write this journal? *(while on Magellan's ship)* Discuss why primary sources are so important to historians. *(The writer may be an eyewitness to events, the writings are descriptions of what existed at the time.)* What kind of source is *A History of US? (a secondary source)* Note that secondary sources often include quotations from primary sources. INFERRING

Meeting Individual Needs
English Language Learners

Students may benefit by listening to Pigafetta's journal read aloud. Then ask students to draw a scene to illustrate the text. As they display their drawings, ask them to retell the story of the scene in their own words.

What's in a Name?

A German mapmaker who was fascinated by the writings of the explorer Amerigo Vespucci wrote the letters *A-M-E-R-I-C-A* on South America, which Vespucci first recognized was a continent. This is how these continents came to be named after Vespucci—not Columbus.

ASK

1. How do we know about Vespucci's travels? *(He wrote letters about them.)*
2. Why did Vespucci call South America a "New World?" *(He realized that this land wasn't China, and it was too big to be the islands of Asia.)*
3. Why did the mapmaker Waldseemuller write AMERICA on his map? *(because Amerigo Vespucci had written about it.)*

 Ponder
What new explorations might change your view of the world or the universe?

 Question Chart

DISCUSS

1. The author says that Vespucci was more open-minded than Columbus, which allowed Vespucci to see South America for what it was: a continent. Have students reread pages 83–84. Ask: Do you agree with the author's evaluation? *(Yes, Columbus had found South America but he couldn't believe it was a continent because he was so focused on finding China.)*
2. Do you think Vespucci's writings would encourage exploration in South America the same way that Marco Polo's book interested people in China? *(Polo's book might have been more inspiring since it described great riches; the America that Vespucci described might have seemed dangerous, but curious and brave people would want to go there.)*
3. Why might Europeans have been so interested in reading Vespucci's descriptions of the people he found? *(Vespucci wrote about very unusual behaviors and activities of the people he encountered in his travels.)*

WRITE

Have students suppose they've read about the adventures of Amerigo Vespucci. They would like to accompany him on his next voyage. In a letter to Vespucci, they should tell him why they are interested in joining his crew.

L I T E R A C Y   L I N K S

Words to Discuss

continent   **Antarctic**

Have students use the dictionary to write definitions of each word and then locate the continents and the Antarctic on the map on pages 178-179. Ask students to name each continent.

Reading Skills
Summarizing

Have students summarize Vespucci's contributions to Europeans' knowledge of the world. Remind them to include only main ideas, not minor details. *(Vespucci identified and described the South American continent, found the Amazon River, and told Europeans about an unfamiliar people, the Patagonians.)*
SYNTHESIZING

Skills Connection
Geography

Have students look at Waldseemuller's map on pages 94-95. Then have them turn to the world map on pages 178-179. Ask them to write a brief report on Waldseemuller's work. What did he get right? What did he get wrong?

THINKING ABOUT THE THEMES

The following questions will help students relate the book's themes to the content of Part 3. You may wish to use the questions for classroom discussion or have students answer them in written form.

1. What diverse ethnic or racial groups were brought together in the Americas in the 30 years following Columbus's first voyage? *(diverse Native American peoples, Spaniards, Africans, Portuguese, Italians, English, and others)*

2. This period saw the movement of European explorers to the "New World." What were the main goals and achievements of the explorations of Columbus, Cabot, Balboa, Magellan, and Vespucci? *(All of the explorers wanted to find the western route to Asia and to find riches. Columbus was the first to reach the Caribbean. Cabot explored the North American coast. Balboa crossed Panama to the Pacific. Magellan led an expedition that was the first to circle the globe. Vespucci identified South America as a continent.)*

3. Draw students' attention to the other themes that have been posted around the room. Give them the opportunity to explore the relevance of these themes to Part 3. Accept choices that are supported by sound reasoning.

ASSESSING PART 3

Use Check-Up 3 (TG page 67) to assess student learning.

NOTE FROM JOY HAKIM

I'm sure you've noticed that these books are written on several levels. The main story is relatively easy reading. Some of the boxed material and some of the margin notes are quite sophisticated. I don't intend for every student to read everything.

PROJECTS AND ACTIVITIES

▶ Advertising the Gutenberg Bible

Assign groups of students to design advertisements that Gutenberg might have used to announce his new printing service. Remind them that many people could not read at the time. Both pictures and words should be used to get across the message of the ads.

▶ Speech! Speech!

Using information from the From Columbus's Pen feature on page 79, students can prepare short speeches in which a returning Columbus addresses the people of Seville. The speeches should tell of all that he saw—and what he failed to see.

▶ Debating the Issue

Use the following topic to stimulate a debate.
Resolved   That Columbus should be honored as one of the great heroes in history. *(This is a hotly debated question. To provoke discussion, you might appoint some students to speak for the Taino.)*

▶ Geographic Dictionary

Have students create a geographic dictionary using geography terms from Parts 1-3. Assign one Part to each of three groups. Have students write each word and definition on an index card and arrange the cards alphabetically. Students can add to the dictionary as they continue reading Book 1.

★★ FACTS TO SHARE ★★

Tales of long-ago happenings sometimes come to us from stories that are passed down orally from generation to generation until eventually someone writes them down. One story from the Hopi people of the Southwest began this way: *"In ancient times it was prophesied . . . that this island would be occupied by the Indian people and then from somewhere a White man would come."*

Clash of Cultures

In 1519, a man rushed to the Aztec emperor with a message. A historian wrote: *He went directly to the palace and said to him [Moctezuma]: "When I went to the shores of the great sea [Gulf of Mexico], there was a . . . small mountain floating in the midst of the water . . . My lord, we have never seen the like of this. . . . "* The mountain was a Spanish ship. Part 4 tells of the conflicts caused by the Spanish arrival in the Americas.

SETTING GOALS

The goals for students in Part 4 are to:
- learn about the beliefs of Europeans and Native Americans in the 1500s.
- describe the roles of Hernando Cortés, Ponce de León, and Pizarro in creating New Spain.
- analyze the ethics of the Spaniards' actions.

GETTING INTERESTED

1. Discuss the idea of religious freedom and ask students to name the diverse religions that exist in the United States today. Ask: How has religious intolerance affected the movement of peoples to the United States? *(People seeking religious freedom have often moved here.)*

2. Have students read the captions and study the illustrations on page 97 and on page 99. Ask: What do these pictures show about the religious beliefs held by the Spanish and the Aztecs at that time? *(For both the Spanish and the Aztecs, killing was an accepted practice in their religious system.)*

Working with Timelines
Tell students that Part 4 covers roughly the years 1513-1533. Have students begin a chronology, writing the important dates in order to sequence the events in this part. (Students may work individually or with partners.) Explain that these decades, terrible for Native Americans, probably would have been described by the Spaniards as glorious. For each chronological entry, have students note the consequences to the native peoples and the actions of the Spanish.

Using Maps
Refer students to the map on page 105 and have them locate the Gulf of Mexico and Tenochtitlán. Ask them to use the title, words, arrow symbols, and drawings to predict what story this map tells. Then have students use a wall map of the world to find the coast of Mexico. Ask students to predict who Cortés was, and why he went to Mexico.

About Beliefs and Ideas

In the 16th century, it was common for people to go to war over their beliefs. Slavery and torture were also common practices around the world. When the Spanish moved into the New World, one of their goals was to convert native peoples to their Catholic religion. The clash between Spaniards and Native Americans was brutal and deadly.

ASK

1. How did the Protestants get their name? *(They were people who protested against some of the ideas of the Catholic Church.)*

2. In Europe, what two religious groups clashed and fought? *(Protestants and Catholics)* What happened to the Jews in Spain? *(If Jews didn't convert to Catholicism, they had to leave Spain or be killed.)*

3. How did some European explorers feel they could best serve God? *(by converting Native Americans to Christianity)* What did they do to people who resisted? *(killed them)* What were some practices of Native Americans at that time? *(blood sacrifice, torture, and slavery)*

4. What was the Inquisition? *(the Spanish religious court that forced non-Catholics to convert or leave Spain)*

DISCUSS

1. What are some possible reasons that Martin Luther wanted to reform the Catholic Church? *(He may have disagreed with religious intolerance and the practices of the Inquisition; he may have been against religious wars.)*

2. Many people in the 16th century believed that their religion was the only "true" one. What did this often lead to? *(People went to war to impose their religious beliefs on others.)*

3. How did religious conflicts play a role in the settlement of the Americas? What right did people first have in the United States? *(Many people came to the Americas to escape these conflicts; the right to religious freedom.)*

WRITE

Ask students which 16th century practices or beliefs they would have opposed. Have them write an open letter to be read at a town meeting that protests these practices. The reasons for their opposition may be religious, moral, or humanitarian.

◉ Ponder
How would you react if someone tried to change your religious beliefs? What can happen to a society when some people think their religion is the *only* right one?

☑ Question Chart

L I T E R A C Y   L I N K S

Words to Discuss

religious war	culture
reformer	convert
Reformation	

Use context to discuss the words. Ask: What is the difference between "changing your mind" and "being converted?" *(Converted means changing a belief or a truth that you hold; changing your mind means making a different decision.)*

Reading Skills
Interpreting Primary Sources

Discuss the role of creation myths and then read aloud the text of the Popol Vuh on page 100. Explain that readers may gain different impressions from reading the same text. Ask the following questions. INFERRING

- What idea is expressed by *Only the sky was? (At one time, only the sky existed.)*

- What synonym might be used for *silence? (the void, nothing, emptiness)*

- Who were the Mayan gods? *Creator and Maker)*

Skills Connection
Philosophy

Use the questions that the author says philosophers ask to have a debate over whether we in the 21st century can judge people of the past:

- Suppose you are convinced that your way of thinking is good for everyone. Can you be sure you are right?

- Are you bad if you do something wrong but you don't know better?

New Spain

Two worlds came together in 1519 when the Spaniards and Aztecs met on a causeway leading into the Aztec city of Tenochtitlán. The conquest of the Aztecs by the conquistador Hernando Cortés resulted in power and glory for the Spanish and death and destruction for the Aztecs.

ASK

1. Who did the Aztecs believe that Cortés might be when they first saw him? Why? *(A god; their calendar predicted a god would come on the same day Cortés arrived.)*
2. How did the Indian woman Doña Marina help Cortés? *(by translating the Aztec language for the Spanish)*
3. What beliefs caused the Aztecs to make human sacrifices? *(They believed that the gods would cause earthquakes and other disasters if they did not make human sacrifices.)* Which people did they sacrifice? *(sons and daughters of neighboring peoples)*
4. What was the outcome of Cortés's assault on Tenochtitlán? *(The Spanish destroyed the city and built Mexico City. They kept the riches they found or sent them to Spain.)*

 Ponder
Would you have shown mercy to somebody like Cuauhtemoc? Why or why not?

✔ **Question Chart**

DISCUSS

1. What were some of the accomplishments of the Aztecs? *(complex political system, magnificent capital, canals and bridges, accurate calendar, arts, music, poetry and crafts)*
2. How big was the Aztec army? *(200,000 men)* How many people traveled with Cortés? *(900)* What are some reasons that Cortés was able to conquer the Aztecs? *(the Aztecs' belief that Cortés was a god, translations by Dona Mariña, horses and guns, help of Indians who hated the Aztecs, smallpox killing many Indians)*
3. Have students begin to complete Resource 8 (TG page 80), which compares the Aztec and Inca civilizations.
4. **Sourcebook:** Read aloud from Source #3 as students follow along. Have them point out how Fray Bernardino de Sahagun shows sympathy for the suffering of the Aztecs.

WRITE

Ask students to write a description of the city of Tenochtitlán and its attractions, using the text and the illustrations. Have them comment on the skills and creativity that were necessary to build such a city.

L I T E R A C Y   L I N K S

Words to Discuss

covet   causeway
artisan   subdue
immunity

After reviewing the vocabulary, have partners write questions that can be answered with one of the vocabulary words. Then have them exchange questions with other pairs and answer the questions.

Reading Skills
Understanding Rhetorical Devices

Explain that the author sometimes poses questions—and doesn't answer them. The answers—not necessarily "right" or "wrong"—will vary with each individual. Have students find examples of such questions in this chapter. Ask: Why is it important to consider a range of opinions about what is right and wrong? *(People have different beliefs and viewpoints that should be respected.)* SYNTHESIZING

Skills Connection
Using Reference Sources

Discuss that students can use many different sources to learn about history. Display *The History of Us Sourcebook* and explain that it contains primary sources about American history. Have them turn to page 10 and discuss the author's notes before reading Source #3.

Ponce de Léon, Pizarro, and Spanish Colonies

Dreams of finding another rich Aztec empire to conquer drove the conquistadors deeper into the Americas. The brutal conquest of the Incan empire centered in Peru by Francisco Pizarro did not quench Spain's thirst for gold.

ASK

1. What did Ponce de Léon win for Spain? What did he never find? *(He got control of Puerto Rico and claim to what is now Florida; he never found the Fountain of Youth.)*

2. What did Pizarro win? *(control of Peru, a fortune in gold and silver)*

3. What happened to the Inca ruler Atahualpa in Cuzco? *(Pizarro killed him even though he had promised not to if the Indians filled a room with gold and silver.)*

4. Why did most Europeans accept the destruction of Native American civilizations? *(Their religion told them that Native Americans were pagans, their religion should be destroyed.)*

Ponder
How could the Incas, without modern tools, have created structures with the massive blocks of stone found at the ruins?

Question Chart

DISCUSS

1. Describe the characters of Ponce de Léon and Pizarro. *(greedy, cruel, brutal)*

2. Pizarro melted down the gold and silver artifacts of the Incas. What does that suggest about what he valued? *(Pizarro placed no value on Inca civilization or the artistic items they produced; he only wanted the precious metals.)*

3. Do you think the Inca civilization would have been destroyed if the Incas had agreed to become Catholics? *(Students should recognize that Pizarro may have acted in the same way, and that converting to Catholicism would have produced great changes in, if not destruction of, Incan civilization.)*

4. Have students continue working on Resource 8 (TG page 80).

WRITE

Ask students to write a poem expressing their feelings about the loss of the Inca civilization. The poem should use information found in the text.

L I T E R A C Y   L I N K S

Words to Discuss

fervently   pagan

Have students look up the words in a dictionary. The margin note on page 111 says that explorers sought gold *fervently*. Ask: Who else in this book has looked for something fervently? Can you use *fervently* to describe some action of yours?

Reading Skills
Analyzing Point of View

Have students find words the author uses to describe Pizarro. *(daring, terrible, deceitful)* Then ask: VISUALIZATION

● What does the author's choice of words suggest about her opinion of Pizarro? *(She has a negative opinion.)*

● What images do the words bring to your mind? *(Responses will vary.)*

● Have students find descriptive words about Inca artifacts on page 113. Ask: Does the author admire the Incans' skills? What images do her descriptions bring to mind?

Skills Connection
History/Math

Explain that the Inca communicated over a vast empire without a system of writing. They used quipu, a system of knotting colored strings to record numerical information. Students can learn more about quipu by visiting the library or going online to such sites as *http://www.spanish.sbc.edu/ MMLatAm/Quipus.html.*

Gloom, Doom, and a Bit of Cheer

Although millions of Indians died due to disease and war, their cultures survived the era of the conquistadors. Over time, Spanish, Indian and African peoples intermarried, bringing a new diversity of people to America.

ASK

1. How did European diseases affect the Native American population of Mexico? *(An estimated three quarters of the 20 million Mexican people died, many due to disease.)*

2. What was the outcome of Cortés's conquest of Mexico? *(Mexico became a colony of Spain.)*

3. Why was there never a United States of South America? *(The colonies were not friendly with each other; they were not linked by roads; gold wasn't found in the north; Portugal and other nations besides Spain created colonies there.)*

4. What changes did the Spaniards bring to the Americas? *(They brought their religion, an end to human sacrifices, their architecture and language, universities, printing presses, ethnic changes through intermarriage.)*

5. Have students complete Resource 9 (TG page 81).

⊙ Ponder
How different would history have been if the Indians had traveled to Europe instead of the Europeans landing in North America?

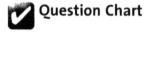 **Question Chart**

DISCUSS

1. Why does the author call the diseases brought by the Europeans "accidents?" *(Europeans didn't know how diseases spread or how to prevent them.)*

2. Which group probably held power in the early colonial days in Mexico: Spaniards, mestizos, or mulattos? *(Spaniards; they were the colonists and as conquerors they had more power.)*

WRITE

Have students write a dialogue between a 16th-century Native American and a Spaniard who has recently arrived in the Americas. Each is trying to convince the other to adapt to his or her way of life. Students may work in pairs or individually.

LITERACY LINKS

Words to Discuss

mestizo	epidemic
mulatto	colony
plague	

Have students use context to discuss the words. Ask: Which words describe people? *(mestizo, mulatto)* Which words are related to the spread of disease? *(plague, epidemic)*

Reading Skills
Understanding Rhetorical Devices

Explain that an analogy makes a comparison. What analogy does the author make to explain why Spain was the "mother country" to Mexico? *(The conquerors were like parents; the colonies were like children.)* Discuss: How does the comparison help you understand the relationship between a colony and a ruling country? *(It explains who has the power.)* Invite students to create their own analogies. INFERRING

Skills Connection
Geography

Direct students to read the margin note on page 115. Then have them use a classroom wall map of the world or an atlas to locate Brazil and the other three countries in South America where Spanish is not the main language. *(Guyana—English; Surinam—Dutch; French Guiana—French)*

THINKING ABOUT THE THEMES

The following questions will help students relate the book's themes to the content of Part 4. You may wish to use the questions for classroom discussion or have students answer them in written form

, When the Spaniards came to the "new world," what changes did they bring? *(New plants and animals, as well as diseases, came from Europe; the Aztec and Inca cultures were largely destroyed; the population became more diverse and included mestizo and mulatto people, Africans, and Spaniards.)*

, What role did religious beliefs play in the conflict between the Spaniards and the Indians? *(Spaniards believed that Catholicism was the true religion and thought the Indians were pagan; some Indians made human sacrifices as part of their religion, which reinforced the Spaniard's view.)*

, Draw students' attention to the other themes that have been posted around the room. Give them the opportunity to explore the relevance of these themes to Part 4. Accept choices that are supported by sound reasoning.

ASSESSING PART 4

Use Check-Up 4 (TG page 68) to assess student learning.

NOTE FROM JOY HAKIM

I want your children to learn words from this book and to learn to love words, too. I'd like to see them become word detectives and go off sleuthing in the "word derivation forest."

PROJECTS AND ACTIVITIES

▶ Create a Skit
Have students work in groups to write the dialogue for a skit that reflect Cortés's and Moctezuma's thoughts and actions before the fighting began. In addition to these leaders, characters should include Dona Mariña, Jeronimo de Aguilar, Maria de Estrada, and Aztec messengers. Have students write two scenes. Have groups perform their skits for the class.

▶ Mural of Mexico—Past and Present
Tell students that a plaque marks the site of the Aztec surrender. It reads in part: "It was neither a triumph nor a defeat: it marked the painful birth of the mestizo nation that Mexico is today." Have students work in groups to help create a mural that includes the plaque and shows scenes of both Aztec culture and present-day Mexico.

▶ News Report
Have students suppose that they are reporting on one of the events in this chapter. Ask students to write a news story that answers questions *Who? What? When? Where? Why?* News stories should include a headline, date, and the location of the event.

▶ Timeline
Have students check their chronology against the one shown on page 167, verifying important dates. Point out that their chronologies will have additional dates and events. Then ask students to use their chronology to write a summary of the events that contributed to the establishment of New Spain.

★★ **FACTS TO SHARE** ★★

The Aztec calendar was based on the cycles of Venus, which takes about 584 days to transform from morning star to evening star. Five of these cycles equal eight sun years. Based on the solar calendar, the Aztec calendar lost a quarter of a day every year. So, every fifty-two years, the Aztecs corrected their calendar by adding thirteen days. An Aztec calendar carved in stone in 1497 is a famous symbol of Mexico. Found in 1760 buried under the main square of Mexico City, it is now in the Museum of Archaeology.

The March North

In 1593, the words of Fray Marcos de Niza spread through Mexico City "I saw . . . seven settlements of fair size. . . . I was informed that in it is much gold, and that the natives . . trade in vessels and jewels. . . ." Such rumors sent the Spanish marching north out of Mexico and the Caribbean. Once again, conflicts occurred as Native Americans tried to fight off the Spanish. Part 5 tells us the story of their struggle.

SETTING GOALS

The goals for students in Part 5 are to:
- discover how the thirst for gold led the Spanish on expeditions from Florida through California.
- discuss the work of missionaries and Bartolomé de Las Casas.
- learn of the brutal treatment of Native Americans by the Spaniards.

GETTING INTERESTED

1. Read aloud this Zuñi description of the Spanish conquistadors: "They wore coats of iron, and warbonnets of metal, and carried for weapons short canes that spit fire and made thunder . . . these . . . people drove our ancients about like slave creatures." Ask students to preview the pictures in Chapters 25-29 that support details in this account. Discuss: Does this description seem accurate? *(The pictures seem to support this view from the perspective of the Zuñi.)*

2. Read the title of Chapter 25, *North of New Spain*. Ask: Where was New Spain? *(Mexico)* What land is north of Mexico? *(present-day United States)* Ask students to predict the answers to these questions: Why did the Spaniards push North? Did religion play a part in their explorations?

Working with Timelines

Have students create a timeline to record the Spanish expeditions into North America in the 1540s. Students should divide their timelines into 10 parts, write the dates, identify the explorers or expeditions, and tell the lands the explorers reached. Have students add information to the timeline after reading each chapter.

Using Maps

Have students turn to the map on page 123. Ask: What does this map tell about the next phase of Spanish exploration? *(The Spaniards are moving north from New Spain.)* Have students trace the routes of De Soto, Cabrillo, and Coronado on this map. Then ask them to use the map of the United States on pages 180-181 to find what present-day locations the explorers passed through.

North of New Spain

After the Spanish had seen the awe-inspiring Aztec and Inca empires, no stories of golden cities seemed too impossible to believe. The Spaniards were convinced that the seven cities of gold were in North America, and set out from New Spain to find them.

ASK

1. Why did Spanish explorers push north from Mexico to explore North America? *(They hoped to find the legendary cities of gold such as Cibola.)*

2. What lands did Narvaez's expedition reach? *(Florida)* Why did his expedition fail? *(He treated the Indians badly; he and many of his men were killed by the Indians.)*

3. Why was Estebán a good choice to lead an expedition to the north? *(He had been with Narvaez in Florida, had lived among the Indians, and had walked from Texas to Mexico. Which Spanish priest was the other expedition leader? (Fray Marcos)*

4. Have students identify the lands of the Zuñi and Apalachee on the map on Resource 3 (TG page 74).

5. Have students complete a Biographical Profile of Estebán on Resource 10 (TG page 82).

Ponder
What reasons might Fray Marcos have had for reporting in Mexico City that Ceuola was "the greatest city in the world"?

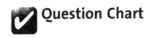

Question Chart

DISCUSS

1. Why do you think it took Estebán and Cabeza de Vaca eight years to walk from Texas to Mexico? *(They probably had no maps and weren't sure where they were going.)* What might their journey have been like? *(They probably endured many hardships along the way.)*

2. How do you think Fray Marcos probably influenced the history of Spanish exploration in North America? *(He reported to Mexico City that the golden cities, including Ceuola, had been found, although he had not seen them; the Spanish thought that Ceuola was Cibola, and they would send many more expeditions to North America.)*

WRITE

After Estebán spent eight years getting back to Mexico, the Spanish governor asked him to set out on another exploring mission. Have students write a letter that Estebán might have sent to the governor responding to this request.

L I T E R A C Y   L I N K S

Words to Discuss

legend   **scout**
pious

Have students use context to determine the meaning of the words and then use a dictionary to check their definitions. Discuss: Why was Cibola a legendary city? *(It was not real.)* Why might a pious person like Fray Marcos feel that someone like Estebán, who liked to dance and sing, was strange? *(Responses will vary.)*

Reading Skills
Previewing Illustrations

Before students read the chapter, have them preview the illustrations. Have them note the details of the appearance and equipment used by the Spanish and compare it to the appearance and dress of the Native Americans. Then have them write questions that they want answered from reading the chapter.
QUESTIONING

Meeting Individual Needs
Enrichment

Ask Spanish-speaking students to help the class pronounce the Spanish words and proper names in Part 5. Students may want to begin a glossary of Spanish words that have become part of the English language.

Looking for Cibola with Coronado

Francisco Vasquez de Coronado believed Fray Marcos's tale about a golden city. In 1540, Coronado's search for Cibola led him on a 7,000-mile journey north from Mexico and across the Southwest, to lands long inhabited by Native Americans.

ASK

1. How was Coronado's expedition different from earlier expeditions in the Southwest? *(It was well planned, well supplied, and included men, women, children, and non-Spaniards, who were treated well.)*

2. How did Coronado and his men treat Indians? *(When the Spaniards wanted food, they kicked Indians out of their pueblo and fought them; they killed the Turk.)*

3. What are some places and landforms that Coronado saw? *(Arizona, New Mexico, Kansas, the Grand Canyon, mountains, plains, quicksand, the Rio Grande)*

4. Why were Coronado and the other soldiers angry with Fray Marcos? *(Ceuola was a group of villages, not one of the Seven Cities of Gold. They said Fray Marcos lied.)*

◉ Ponder
Why do you think Mexican Indians and other non-Spaniards might have wanted to go on Coronado's expedition? What did they hope to find?

✔ Question Chart

DISCUSS

1. Why do you think many Indians told Coronado's expedition that the golden cities were just a few days away? *(It was a good way to avoid conflict; they told Coronado what he wanted to hear.)*

2. What might it have been like to be a conquistador? What character traits would a person need? *(Conquistadors would need courage, strength, fighting skills, knowledge of languages, the ability to make maps, and the ability to make decisions.)*

WRITE

Have students suppose they are among Coronado's explorers who have returned to Mexico after the expedition failed. They are to write a journal entry telling whether or not they would join a future expedition.

LITERACY LINKS

Words to Discuss

mythological

Have students look up *mythological* in the dictionary. Help them to draw a connection between *legendary* and *mythological* and then ask them to write a sentence that includes the word *mythological*.

Reading Skills
Using Text Features

Elicit that the main idea of the chapter is Coronado's search for Cibola. Refer to the margin notes on pages 120-121. Explain that they contain information related to, but not essential to, the text. When students encounter margin notes, encourage them to consider why the information is included. Ask: What is the purpose of the margin notes in this chapter? *(to give interesting facts about Indian cultures encountered by Coronado)*
QUESTIONING

Skills Connection
Geography

Have students turn to the map on page 123 and locate the triangle symbol that identifies the town where Coronado started his journey. *(Compostela)* Ask: What symbol shows the route of his journey? *(a dashed line)* Have students name other symbols on the map and list the information shown on the map. *(dates and routes of explorations, etc.)*

Conquistadors: California to Florida

In the 1540s, Spanish conquistadors came to North America. They landed in Florida, moving west across what is now Texas into New Mexico and Arizona. Others reached California by sea. In their search for gold, the conquistadors caused great suffering among Native Americans, and the Indians often fought back.

ASK

1. What did the voyages of Alarcon and Cabrillo teach the Spanish about the land of California? *(It was not an island, but a huge landmass.)*

2. What did De Soto learn about the land on his westward journey from Florida? What did he learn about Native Americans? *(He found the Mississippi; the dense Indian populations in the Southeast, the guerrilla fighting methods of the Apalachee, the customs of the Natchez.)*

3. Using Resource 11 (TG page 83), have students identify the Spanish explorers' routes and complete the chart.

DISCUSS

1. Since De Soto admired the Inca ruler Atahualpa and was dismayed when Pizarro killed him, why do you think De Soto killed so many Indians? *(He was searching for gold, and would fight anyone who stood in his way.)*

2. Why were the guerrilla fighting methods of the Native Americans so effective? *(They hid and ambushed the conquistadors; there were no open battlefields where they would have probably been killed by European weapons.)*

3. Indians in Texas correctly told De Soto that there were "other men that speak as they do" not far away. What might this suggest about the communication network among different Native American peoples? *(Possible response: Native American peoples who lived in different areas probably had contact with each other.)*

⊚ Ponder
Native Americans allowed the Africans and Spaniards who left De Soto's expedition to join their tribes. Why do you think they did this?

✓ Question Chart

WRITE

Have students write a dialogue that might have taken place between De Soto and Coronado if they had met. What geographical information could they have exchanged?

L I T E R A C Y   L I N K S

Words to Discuss

lance   hostage
guerrilla

Have students make a word web with *Warfare* at the center. Have them put the vocabulary words in circles around the center, and write a sentence explaining how each word applies to *Warfare*.

Reading Skills
Using Time Order

Recall for students that the author states that the race was on to find Cibola. Explain that this chapter is organized in time order so that readers can use dates to understand when explorations began, ended, or overlapped. Ask the following questions. SYNTHESIZING

- In what year did Alarcon begin his journey? *(1540)* Cabrillo? *(1542)*

- When did De Soto's journey begin? *(1539)* How long did the expedition last? *(4 years)*

Skills Connection
Math

Using a large map of North America, have students identify the routes of De Soto, Cabeza de Vaca, Coronado, and others shown on the map on page 123. Point out that Coronado traveled about 7,000 miles. Have students use the map scale and a ruler to estimate the length of each of the other journeys.

A Place Called Santa Fe

A violent silver baron named Juan de Oñate started a Spanish colony in North America. After he was called back to Mexico, members of his expedition founded the settlement of Santa Fe. Soon, Spanish missionaries and more settlers arrived in the first permanent European colony in the North American West.

ASK

1. Why was Juan de Oñate's expedition important? *(It founded the first European colony in the present-day Southwest.)* Why was the settling of Santa Fe important? *(It became the first permanent European colony.)*

2. Name two ways that the arrival of the Spanish affected Native Americans. *(Some Indians converted to Christianity. Many more died of European and African diseases.)*

3. Why was Juan de Oñate forced to leave his settlement and return to Mexico City? *(He behaved badly toward the Indians; he was recalled by the government.)*

 Ponder
Why do you think the explorers felt it was worthwhile to try so hard to find gold?

✔ **Question Chart**

DISCUSS

1. How was the population in what is now the United States becoming more diverse? *(People from Mexico, including Spaniards, Africans, mestizos, and mulattos, began to move north to settle in New Mexico.)*

2. Explain why you think the missionaries in Santa Fe were either successful or unsuccessful. *(Successful: They converted 60,000 Indians to Catholicism. Unsuccessful: Many Indians who converted continued to practice their native religions.)*

WRITE

Have students suppose they are with Oñate in Santa Fe. They are to write a letter to a friend in Spain, describing their experience. What do they think of Oñate? Do they want to stay or to leave?

LITERACY LINKS

Words to Discuss

missionary	ritual
mission	practice

Have students use a dictionary as well as context to determine the meaning of the words. Ask them also to recall the meaning of *convert*. Discuss: What do the four words have in common? What is the goal of a missionary?

Reading Skills
Evaluating Persuasive Devices

Have students list words the author uses to tell what Oñate did to the Acoma Indians *(seizes, slaughters, enslaves)* Ask the following questions. ANALYZING

• How do the words support the author's statement that "Oñate is a dreadful man?" *(All the words bring up images of terrible things.)*

• How do these words persuade readers that her view is correct? *(These are not words that are used to describe a good person.)*

Meeting Individual Needs
Visual Learners

Encourage students to use the information in paragraph 4 on page 129 to draw a picture of Oñate's expedition. Then ask them to use their picture to explain the people, animals, and goods that traveled with Oñate to New Mexico.

Las Casas Cares

The priest Bartolomé de Las Casas was an outspoken defender of the Native American peoples and of human rights. His protest against harsh Spanish policies and Indian slavery sparked a heated debate among Spanish people.

ASK

1. What work did Indians and black slaves do for the Spaniards? *(Indians: gold and silver mining, farming: black slaves: growing tobacco and sugarcane)*
2. What actions did Las Casas take to try to prevent the harsh treatment of the Indians? *(He delivered sermons, wrote books, started "towns of free Indians," founded Venezuela as a place where different races might work together, advised the king, and wrote laws.)*
3. What effect did Las Casas's argument have on King Charles I of Spain? *(The king outlawed Indian slavery.)*

DISCUSS

1. How would you describe Las Casas's main goal in establishing "towns of free Indians?" *(He wanted to create a place where people from all cultures would live as equals.)* What would Las Casas have thought about our Constitution? *(He would have agreed with its principles.)*
2. What was Sepulveda's argument for Indian slavery? *(He believed that it was "natural" for some people to be masters and some people to be slaves.)*
3. A book by Las Casas was found in which he wrote: "To these quiet lands . . . came the Spaniards . . . with a sharp and tedious hunger." What did he mean? *(The Spaniards, with their unquenchable thirst for adventure and gold, had been a destructive force in the New World.)*

Ponder
If Las Casas's colony in Venezuela had been successful, do you think the early colonies in North America would have been run differently?

 **Question Chart**

WRITE

Ask students to write a letter to Bartolomé de Las Casas, telling the priest what they think of his ideas about Spain's treatment of the Native Americans.

LITERACY LINKS

Words to Discuss

sovereign   unjust
subject   inferior
injustice   superior

After finding the meanings of the words in the dictionary, ask students: What do the prefixes *un-* and *in-* mean? *(not)* Which two pairs of words are antonyms? *(sovereign/subject; inferior/superior)* Which class of people was thought to be superior? *(sovereigns)* Which class was thought to be inferior? *(subjects)*

Reading Skills
Comparing and Contrasting

Have students create two compare-and-contrast charts that analyze:

- Las Casas's actions and beliefs before and after delivering his sermon in 1514. Points of comparison should include ideas about enslavement of Indians and religious influences.
- Las Casas's and Sepulveda's arguments on Indian enslavement. Points should include opinions, personal background, influences, and effects of each man's arguments. ANALYZING

Meeting Individual Needs
Reteaching

Have students use the illustrations on pages 133-135 to explain the work that enslaved Indians and Africans did for the Spanish.

THINKING ABOUT THE THEMES

The following questions will help students relate the book's themes to the content of Part 5. You may wish to use the questions for classroom discussion or have students answer them in written form.

1. How did the movement of the conquistadors and the missionaries into North America increase the diversity of the population? *(Besides the Spanish, there were Mexicans, mulattos, mestizos, and Africans who joined expeditions; some of these people stayed in North America; the missionaries were Spanish, and increased the Spanish population.)*

2. In what ways did Estéban and some other Africans and Spaniards adapt to the Americas and to Native American cultures? *(They learned the local languages, adapted to customs, developed survival skills; some intermarried.)*

3. In what ways did the Spanish conquistadors adapt in North America? *(They adapted to new foods and some of the fighting methods used by the Indians.)*

4. Draw students' attention to the other themes that have been posted around the room. Give them the opportunity to explore the relevance of these themes to Part 5. Accept choices that are supported by sound reasoning.

ASSESSING PART 5

Use Check-Up 5 (TG page 69) to assess student learning.

NOTE FROM JOY HAKIM

I've been a teacher and I believe that there is nothing more important in the school years than producing good readers. If students learn to read well—even if they forget the details of the subject matter—they will have a lifetime skill that will allow them to learn on their own.

PROJECTS AND ACTIVITIES

▶ Designing Story Boards

Have students work in small groups to illustrate key events in the story of the expedition of Panfilo de Narvaez. Ask them to write captions for their drawings, and to arrange them in sequence in a display.

▶ Interview with a Conquistador

Divide the class into small groups. In each group, have some students write questions for one of the conquistadors discussed in this Part. Have other students write the answers. Then have each group present its "live" interview for the class.

▶ Reenacting History

Have students create a skit in which Juan Ginés de Sepulveda and Bartolomé de Las Casas present their points of view on slavery to King Charles I. The rest of the students, acting as advisors to the king or as friends of Las Casas, can then discuss which person presents the best policy for strengthening Spain.

▶ Fashions of the Times

Ask students to compare the outfits and gear of De Soto and his men with that of the Natchez Indians in Alabama. They may do this either by making a chart and completing it with written descriptions or by making two drawings that illustrate the information found in the text.

★★ FACTS TO SHARE ★★

When Cabeza de Vaca and Estéban met the Spanish slave-hunters in Mexico, the soldiers were speechless. After seven years of wandering in the Southwest, De Vaca seemed neither white nor Indian. Maybe this was because De Vaca had encountered 23 different groups of Native Americans—fought with them, traded with them, been enslaved by them, preached to them, and healed them. Later, back in Spain, De Vaca became a spokesperson for humane treatment of the Indians.

6

Enter the French

For centuries, the Winnebago have passed down the story of their first meeting with the French. One version says: "Then the French . . . came ashore . . . , and the Indians put tobacco in their hands. . . . They did not know what tobacco was. . . . Suddenly a Frenchman saw an old man smoking and poured water on him. . . . After a while they got more accustomed to one another." Part 6 describes the events that led the French onto Native American lands.

SETTING GOALS

The goals for students in Part 6 are to:
- review the role of Spain in Europe and the Americas
- describe the growing conflict between France and Spain in North America
- chart the lands claimed in America by the French

GETTING INTERESTED

1. Read aloud the Winnebago quote on the top of this page. Ask: How does the quote show that the French and Indians may adapt to each other's ways? *(The quote says they became accustomed to one another.)* Do you think the French will get along with the Indians better than the Spaniards did? Why? (Possible response: *The quote suggests that they will.)*

2. During the time of the conquistadors, Spain was the most powerful nation in Europe. Why might other European nations want to go to the Americas? (Possible response: *Other nations might want to get gold from the Americas, too, in order to gain power and money at home, or to establish colonies in other lands.)*

Working with Timelines
Point out to students that index cards can help them keep track of events. As students come across an important event, have them use the card to record the date, the name of the country or countries involved, and a brief description of what happened. After completing Part 6, the class can order the cards by date.

Using Maps
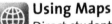
Direct students to the map on page 147. Ask them to locate the key under the title and read the caption. These are some of the people who were leaving their mark in the southeast at that time. Have them turn to the map on page 181 to find the present-day locations of the French and Spanish explorations. How far to the north and south did these nations reach?

The Big Picture

In the 16th century, a flood of gold had made Spain the most powerful nation in Europe. It also proved to be its undoing. Without realizing it, the Spaniards were planting the seeds of their own decline.

ASK

1. What did the Spaniards achieve in the Americas? *(They conquered a huge territory, built cities, helped develop a new way of life.)*
2. What were some of the reasons that Spain had a weak economy? *(There was inflation, taxes went up, people came to the Americas, and Jews and Muslims left as a result of the Inquisition.)*
3. What groups were persecuted by the Inquisition in Spain? *(Jews, Muslims, Protestants, and Catholics who spoke out against the Inquisition)*

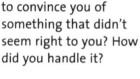 **Ponder**
Has anyone ever tried to convince you of something that didn't seem right to you? How did you handle it?

 **Question Chart**

DISCUSS

1. What were some signs that democracy did not exist in Spain in the 1500s? *(People whose religious beliefs differed from the acceptable ones of the Court and the Catholic Church were tortured and killed; also, Spaniards took slaves to the Americas to work for them.)*
2. Not everyone in Spain believed in Catholicism. What were their choices? *(They could convert or leave the country; if their conversion did not seem sincere, they were killed.)*

WRITE

Note that large plants can grow from small seeds. Ask students to write a paragraph entitled "Seeds of Destruction in Spain," indicating the signs that Spain's problems would grow bigger.

LITERACY LINKS

Words to Discuss

freethinker	heretic
inflation	economy

Have students look up the meaning of *inflation* and *economy* in the dictionary. Have them use the margin note on page 137 to review the meaning of the other words. Ask: Which two words would be considered synonyms in the 1500s? *(freethinker, heretic)* Which words complete this sentence: _____ can hurt a nation's _____. *(inflation, economy)*

Reading Skills
Outlining

Have students or pairs make an outline of Chapter 30. (You may wish to refer them to Resource 4 on TG page 75 to review the form of an outline.) Suggest that they use the title *Spain in the 16th Century*. If needed, suggest main topics such as "Spain's Accomplishments," "Spain's Economy," and "The Inquisition." When students have finished, have them discuss their choices of subtopics and details with other students. ANALYZING

Skills Connection
Evaluating Visual Aids

The picture on page 137 depicts an episode during the Inquisition. Ask students:
- Which groups of people are in charge? *(soldiers and priests)*
- What symbols are being held before the condemned man? *(a cross, a Bible)*
- What does the caption say about Hatuey's beliefs? *(He would rather burn than change his beliefs.)*

From Spain to England to France

In the mid-1500s in Europe, church and state were closely entwined, giving the rulers of nations power over people's religious beliefs. Religious wars in Spain, England, and France raged between Catholics and Protestants. These wars drained treasuries and sent people across the Atlantic to seek religious freedom.

ASK

1. Why did other European nations dislike Spain? *(They were jealous of Spain's power and wealth; Protestant nations opposed the Catholic religion of Spain.)*

2. What religion did King Henry VIII of England establish? Who was its leader? *(The Anglican Church; King Henry)* Whom did the Anglicans persecute? *(English Catholics)*

3. What was the cause of the civil wars in France? *(Religious differences between Catholics and Protestants.)*

4. Have students complete Resource 12 (TG page 84).

 **Ponder**
Why do you think the European leaders were opposed to giving people religious freedom?

✓ **Question Chart**

DISCUSS

1. Why was Queen Mary called "Bloody Mary"? *(A Catholic, she had many Protestants killed.)*

2. How did the religious wars and conflicts in Europe affect the settlement of the Americas? *(People went to the Americas to avoid religious persecution.)*

WRITE

Ask students to suppose that they are young French Protestants. They are to write a diary entry explaining why they are leaving France to go to the Americas.

L I T E R A C Y   L I N K S

Words to Discuss

persecute   civil war

Have students use a dictionary to determine the meaning of the words. Discuss: How can persecution lead to a civil war? What is religious persecution?

Reading Skills
Drawing Conclusions

Tell students that facts in a text can be used to draw conclusions. Point to the following facts stated in the text:

- Henry VIII, king of England, set up a Protestant church and declared himself its leader.

- Queen Mary, a Catholic, tried to make England Catholic again.

- In France, from 1562 to 1598, eight wars were fought over religion. Ask: What conclusion can you draw from these facts? *(Religion was very important in Europe in the 1500s.)* INFERRING

Meeting Individual Needs
Visual Learners

To help students understand the events in the chapter, encourage them to use the dates in the text to make a timeline showing the religious wars that were waged in England and France.

France in America: Pirates and Adventurers

The first French people who arrived in the Americas were explorers and pirates. However, one explorer, Jean Ribaut, established a Huguenot settlement in present-day South Carolina. The settlement failed, but the French did not give up their determination to establish claims in the New World.

ASK

1. Which explorers helped France establish claims in the Americas? *(Verrazano, Cartier and Ribaut.)*

 Ponder
Why do you think the rescue of Ribaut's crew might have caused such interest and excitement in England?

2. Who were the Huguenots? *(French Protestants)* What did Ribaut hope to accomplish by establishing a Huguenot colony in America? *(He wanted to build a place where French Protestants could escape persecution and claim land for France.)*

3. Why did the English catch "New World fever" and become interested in America? *(Ribaut and his men ended up in England and told stories about the riches of America.)*

4. Have students complete Resource 12 (TG page 84) and complete a poster that encourages travel to the New World.

 Question Chart

DISCUSS

1. Why did Ribaut's settlement in Charlesfort fail? *(The men were sailors who were not prepared for farming, they were out of supplies, the Indians stopped giving them food, and the men left Charlesfort to sail back to France.)*

2. Why didn't the French travel to Mexico or South America to get the gold they wanted? *(Spaniards controlled those places; it was easier to steal from the Spanish ships.)*

3. Why did the Florida coast become a base for pirates and privateers? *(Spanish ships traveling from South America with gold passed the coast of Florida on their way to the Gulf Stream. Pirates and privateers laid in wait for them in Florida.)*

WRITE

Have students imagine they are making a movie about privateers or pirates. Have them write a paragraph describing a scene in the film. They should give information about the people, the place, and the riches that are to be captured.

L I T E R A C Y L I N K S

Words to Discuss

privateer Gulf Stream
pirate channel

Have students use the dictionary as well as context to determine the meanings of the words. Discuss: Which pairs of words share something in common? *(privateer, pirate)* What is it? *(They both name people who attack ships for treasure.)*

Reading Skills
Interpreting Figures of Speech

On page 141, read the metaphor *the Gulf Stream . . . is actually a river in the ocean* and the simile *Sailing on the stream is like stepping on a moving belt*. Point out that these comparisons help readers create mental images of the Gulf Stream. Ask: Why is following the Gulf Stream the best route across the Atlantic? *(The current of the Gulf Stream helps the movement of boats.)*
VISUALIZING

Meeting Individual Needs
English Language Learners

Help students understand the similarities and difference between privateers and pirates by modeling a Venn diagram. Have students label the left circle *Pirates*, the right circle *Privateers*, and the overlapping section *Both*, and have students fill in the diagram. *(Privateers: served their nation; split loot with royal treasuries. Pirates: outlaws; kept stolen goods themselves. Both: stole from other ships.)*

Rain, Ambush, and Murder

Spain and England soon followed the French Huguenots to the southeastern coast of North America. There, the three nations battled over control of lands that had long belonged to the Native Americans.

ASK

. Which nation established Fort Caroline? Who fought over it, and why? *(The French; the French and the Spanish fought because they both wanted control of the land and the shipping routes.)*

. Who attacked the Spanish forts Santa Elena and St. Augustine? *(The English captain Francis Drake attacked them.)*

. What were the names that Spain, France, and England gave to southeastern North America? *(La Florida, New France, and Virginia)*

. Have students complete Resource 13 (TG page 85) to understand the riches the pirates and privateers were fighting over.

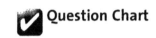**Ponder**
What do you suppose the Indians were thinking while the English, the French, and the Spaniards were battling to settle their homelands?

✔ **Question Chart**

DISCUSS

. How did Menendez's troops manage a surprise attack on the French Fort Caroline? *(The Spaniards marched to Fort Caroline through a hurricane and since the French couldn't imagine being attacked in that weather, no one was on guard.)*

. What do you predict will happen to the Native Americans in the next century, as France, England, and Spain continue to fight over land in the New World? *(They will lose their land and fight with the Europeans.)*

WRITE

Have students write a you-are-there description of the march of Menendez's men from Saint Augustine to Fort Caroline. For their descriptions, have them use information in the chapter, what they may know about hurricanes, and their own imaginations.

L I T E R A C Y   L I N K S

Words to Discuss

swashbuckling   plunder

Have students use a dictionary to determine the meaning of *plunder*. Then ask them to make up a sentence that uses both vocabulary words.

Reading Skills
Evaluating Text Features
Direct students to the Who Am I? feature on page 146. Ask the following questions. ANALYZING

• How did the beaver change? *(It once weighed 800 pounds; over time it became much smaller.)*

• Why are we lucky the beaver still exists today? *(Because of European hunters, they almost became extinct.)*

• Why might the author have included this feature? *(to show how the arrival of Europeans affected a native animal; to warn against exploiting the environment)*

Skills Connection
Geography

Direct students' attention to the map on page 145. Ask: How does this map help you understand the diversity of people in North America in the mid-1500s? *(The map key and the illustrations show that the southeast included Indians, Spanish, and French people.)*

New France

In the 1600s, the French pushed far north into Canada, traveled down the Mississippi, and traded and trapped across Canada to the Great Lakes. The explorer La Salle claimed all the lands west of the Mississippi for France and named the vast area Louisiana.

ASK

1. In what ways did the French adapt to their new environment? *(They hunted beaver, fished, made friends and traded with the Indians.)*
2. Which Indian peoples were friendly with the French? *(Algonquin and Huron)* Who were the enemies of these Indians? *(Iroquois)*
3. What did Samuel de Champlain accomplish? *(He was a fine sailor, writer, artist, and mapmaker. He founded Quebec.)*
4. Why did New France grow so slowly? *(Most French people were happy in France. French Huguenots were not welcome in Catholic Canada.)*

 Ponder
The Indians, who had never seen guns before, called the French weapons "thunderhorns." What does this tell you about the Indians' reaction to guns?

 **Question Chart**

DISCUSS

1. Have students compare the two quotations on page 147. Ask: In the early days, why was trade easy between these Europeans and Indians? *(Each group had goods that the other wanted and valued.)*
2. Read the Traveling by Canoe and Portage feature. Ask: What important discovery did Marquette and Joliet make about the geography of the United States? *(The Mississippi empties into the Gulf of Mexico.)* What lands did La Salle claim for France? *(Canada and the lands west of the Mississippi)*

WRITE

Ask students to write an ad for beaver hats placed in a French newspaper by a hat manufacturer. The ad should create interest by telling something about the Frenchmen who risked danger in the New World.

LITERACY LINKS

Words to Discuss

portage   Jesuit

Have students use information from the text to define the words. Explain that *portage* comes from the French verb *porter*, meaning "to carry." Ask: Why would it have been difficult for Marquette and Joliet to travel by canoe and portage? *(because they often had to carry their canoes)*

Reading Skills
Recognizing Point of View

Elicit that the purpose for the feature on pages 150-151 is to give readers an idea of what the French explorers did. Read the last paragraph and ask these questions. ANALYZING

• What does the author say are the three goals of French exploration? *(find wealth, "civilize" native peoples, bring Christianity)*

• Why do you think the author puts quotation marks around *civilize*? *(From her point of view, the Indians were civilized. From the French point of view, they were not.)*

Skills Connection
Geography

Direct students to the map on page 148. Explain that maps made in earlier times were often illustrated by artists. Have students describe the people, scenes, and events shown on the map. Ask: Why would this map appeal to French missionaries? *(The converted Indian family at the top looks content.)*

THINKING ABOUT THE THEMES

The following questions will help students relate the book's themes to the content of Part 6. You may wish to use the questions for classroom discussion or have students answer them in written form.

How did the movement of Europeans into eastern North America affect Native Americans? *(The Indians often had to fight the Europeans; they lost their land; their human rights were violated.)* How did this movement affect diversity? *(People from Spain, England, France, and Africa mixed with the Native American population.)*

Which Europeans adapted somewhat to Indian ways of life? *(French)* How might this have affected their relations with native peoples? *(It may have helped them get along with the Algonquin, Huron, and Winnebago.)*

Draw students' attention to the other themes that have been posted around the room. Give them the opportunity to explore the relevance of these themes to Part 6. Accept choices that are supported by sound reasoning.

ASSESSING PART 6

Use Check-Up 6 (TG page 70) to assess student learning.

NOTE FROM JOY HAKIM

Learning history helps you think and question and make comparisons. I'm not talking about names and dates and "memorize-dull-details" history. I'm talking about "idea-centered" history. History that grapples with real issues of the past and relates them to problems of today. That is what the best history does and always has done.

PROJECTS AND ACTIVITIES

▶ A Queenly Speech

Ask students to write a brief speech for Elizabeth Tudor to give upon becoming queen of England. Speeches should touch upon both religion and foreign policy.

▶ French Mapmakers

Have students work in small groups to create maps showing the route of exploration taken by Marquette and Joliet or La Salle. They should make a large version of the land area shown on page 151. If possible, have students trace a photocopied enlargement of the map, or provide an opaque projector. Students should include important land features. Encourage them to include drawings (as on the map on page 148) that illustrate the people and events on these journeys.

▶ Indian Conference

Have small groups create a conversation in which Iroquois and Huron leaders discuss their opinions of the French, including their customs, behavior, and skills. Students should write the questions they will pose, and then exchange papers, making notes on their responses to questions of others. Then students can perform their "conferences" for the class.

▶ Timeline

Have partners sort their index cards by date, and notice which cards have overlapping time periods. Have students form groups to compare their cards. Then ask students to construct a timeline of the events they have noted, using time intervals of their own choosing.

★★ FACTS TO SHARE ★★

Louis Joliet was an experienced trader, explorer, and mapmaker. (He had even found time to study for the priesthood.) But even such an accomplished person can have accidents. On his away back from the expedition with Marquette, Joliet's canoe overturned on the St. Lawrence River. All the maps he had made of their journey went overboard. Later, he made maps of their journey from memory!

7

Enter the English

In the late 1500s, England was stirred by the spirit of nationalism. Under Queen Elizabeth, the English prepared to seize an empire from Spain and made plans to move into North America. The great poet Shakespeare reflected the spirit of the times when he wrote, "Hold hard thy breath, and bend up every spirit. . . . On, on you noblest English! . . ." Part tells us about these times.

SETTING GOALS

The goals for students in Part 7 are to:
- explain how the English tried to become the major power in North America.
- discover English motives for colonizing North America.
- learn the difficulties of establishing colonies in North America.

GETTING INTERESTED

1. Have students preview the margin notes on page 157. Ask: The first permanent settlements in North America tell us that which people have moved there? *(The French and Spanish have moved into North America.)* What do you predict might happen between England and these nations when the English move toward North America? *(There will be conflict between the English, French, and Spanish.)*

2. Have students read the title of Chapter 36. Elicit the meaning of *utopia*, or explain that it means "a perfect way of life." Ask: Do you think the English will find utopia in America? Explain. *(Probably not, because the French and Spanish had many problems in America.)*

Working with Timelines

Have students make a timeline on which they can record important dates and events from 1558 through 1600. Working individually or in a group, students may divide the timeline into intervals of their own choosing. Have them take notes of significant events as they read and make entries on the timeline after reading each chapter.

Using Maps

Refer students to a wall map of the world and have them locate England, France, and Spain. Ask: How would you compare the distances that the French, Spanish, and English had to travel to reach America? *(The Spanish were a bit closer; England and France had to travel almost equal distance.)* Ask: How might the locations of these nations affect conflicts that might arise between them? *(Any conflicts would involve ships, since the countries are separated by water.)*

Elizabeth and Friends

The confidence and energy of Queen Elizabeth sparked a new spirit of patriotism among the English. Under this queen, England began to take its place among the great powers of the world.

ASK

. What were some of Elizabeth's achievements or skills? *(musician, poet, spoke French, Spanish, Italian, could read and write Greek and Latin; a great monarch)*

. What was the Elizabethan Age? *(the time in England in the 16ᵗʰ century when Queen Elizabeth ruled)* What were some of the characteristics of the age? *(a time of many cultural achievements)*

. What did the Queen and other political leaders want for England? *(to become the most powerful nation in Europe)*

**Ponder**
What would have been exciting about living in the Elizabethan Age? What would you have disliked about it?

DISCUSS

. Why do you think people might have been especially ready to adopt new ideas and attitudes when Elizabeth came to power? *(Protestants, who had been in danger during Mary's reign, gained freedom when Elizabeth took power. When people have more freedom they are more willing to try new ideas.)*

. What conclusions can you draw about the relations between European nations at this time? *(The Europeans were engaged in a power struggle that would lead to or encourage wars.)*

. What might a dinner with Elizabeth and Sir Walter Raleigh have been like? *(Responses will vary. Students can gather information from the text.)*

✅ **Question Chart**

WRITE

Have students suppose it is the Elizabethan Age. They are to write a friend, inviting that person to a dinner party at Queen Elizabeth's palace. Included in the letter should be suggestions on how to dress and what to expect.

LITERACY LINKS

Words to Discuss

court   chivalry
Elizabethan Age

Have students find the definition of chivalry in the dictionary and reread the margin note about the word court on page 152. Then ask students to construct a word web with Elizabethan Age in the center circle and court and chivalry in the outer circles. Have them brainstorm words that are associated with each word.

Reading Skills
Evaluating Word Choice

Have students identify the words the author uses to describe Queen Elizabeth. *(smart, tough, energetic, the best monarch England ever had)* Ask: ANALYZING

- How do these words influence the readers? *(Readers will have a favorable impression of Elizabeth.)*

- What do the descriptions tell about the writer's evaluation of Elizabeth? *(The author thinks Elizabeth was a great queen.)*

Skills Connection
History/Literature

Point out that accomplishments in literature and the arts are part of what made the Elizabethan Age a great period in English history. It was, for instance, the time of William Shakespeare. Tell students that the play *Romeo and Juliet* was one of Shakespeare's many works. Students who want to find out more about him can go online to **http://www.shakespeare-online.com**.

Utopia in America

Like other Europeans, the English were drawn to North America by dreams of wealth and a new world. But the English also dreamed of establishing a good society in America. Their first attempt at colonization showed them how difficult colonization would be.

ASK

1. Who was Sir Humphrey Gilbert? *(the first Englishman to hold a royal charter for lands in America)* What was unique about the English plans for the settlers? *(The charter said that settlers would lose no English rights in the new land; they would be entitled to trial by jury, the proprietor could not be a dictator.)*

2. What was Sir Thomas More's book *Utopia* about? *(a perfect society on an island)* How did the book inspire Sir Gilbert and Sir Walter Raleigh? *(It encouraged their dream of establishing a good society.)*

3. Who sent the first three English expeditions to America? *(Sir Walter Raleigh)* Why did the first attempts at establishing a colony fail? *(The people got hungry and homesick; they weren't prepared for the difficulty of living in a new land.)*

◎ Ponder
Do you think Sir Thomas More really believed in *Utopia*? (Remind students that in Greek, *utopia* means "no place.")

✔ Question Chart

DISCUSS

1. What were Sir Walter Raleigh's qualifications as a leader? *(He was determined; he sent three expeditions to North America.)* Why was he given the royal charter? *(It had belonged to his brother Sir Gilbert, who died, and Queen Elizabeth was his friend.)*

2. Why might it make sense to try to establish a utopia , or an ideal community, in a new land? *(There are no established customs or systems of government to adapt to; people could set new policies and rules.)*

WRITE

Ask students to write a paragraph entitled "Utopia," describing their vision of an ideal country. Have them include their ideas for government, people's rights, and how the economy would work.

L I T E R A C Y   L I N K S

Words to Discuss

proprietor   utopia
royal charter

Have students read more about these words in the dictionary. Ask: Which word has *landlord* as its synonym? *(proprietor)* What makes a *charter* a "royal charter?" *(It is a grant of rights from a king or queen.)* How are *proprietor* and *royal charter* related? *(The grant of rights over the property is given by the king or queen to the proprietor.)*

Reading Skills
Drawing Conclusions

Direct students to the end of page 156 where the author says that Drake "came by to check on" the colonists. Ask: What questions could you ask about this event? *(Where had Drake been? How did he happen to come by? In what year did this happen?)* Then have students re-read the end of page 144 to the beginning of page 145. Ask: What facts can help you draw conclusions about how Drake happened to "come by? " *(Drake*

attacked Santa Elena in 1586 and then St. Augustine; after that, he probably sailed north to North Carolina where the colonists were located. The colonists had sailed from England in 1585.)
QUESTIONING

Lost: A Colony

Sir Walter Raleigh's third expedition to the New World included women and children. The English colony at Roanoke Island was more than a failure—it was a disaster. Natural events, including drought and rough seas, battles with Spain, and the settlers' inexperience all worked against the English colony.

ASK

1. In what way were the Europeans "arrogant"? *(They thought they were more important than the Native Americans; they believed that America was empty and available for the taking.)*

2. Who was Virginia Dare? *(the first English baby born in America; the granddaughter of John White.)*

3. What happened to the on colony on Roanoke Island? *(It disappeared.)* What did John White find when he returned to the colony from England? *(the letters CRO carved into a tree which White thought might mean that the settlers had gone to Croatan Island)*

4. What mistakes were made by the settlers at Roanoke? *(The colonists were too late to plant crops; they didn't spend enough time looking for food or building houses.)*

⊚ Ponder
Have you ever met someone who is arrogant? What do you think is the best way to handle such a person?

✅ Question Chart

DISCUSS

1. Do you think the English tried hard enough to find the lost settlers of Roanoke? Explain. *(Yes; White did return from England to find them but couldn't stay because a storm forced his ship to sail. In 1603, six Englishmen were killed by Indians on their way to look for the missing people.)*

2. The author asks what lesson can be learned from the effects of the Indians' adoption of the muskets. What would your answer be? *(The musket made the Indians dependent on the English; it allowed the English to divide them; a weapon that supposedly made them more powerful weapon actually made them less powerful.)*

WRITE

Have students prepare a flyer that encourages English settlers to go to America. Have them include the destination and the qualities of a successful settler. Students may wish to include an illustration.

L I T E R A C Y   L I N K S

Words to Discuss

grant	arrogance
breakers	northeaster

Have students use a dictionary to find the meaning of the words. Ask: How is a grant different from a charter? *(A grant is a deed of land; a charter establishes the rights of people.)* What is the possible relationship between a northeaster and breakers? *(A northeaster—a bad storm—can cause very high waves—breakers.)*

Reading Skills
Combining Text and Map Information

Have students read the feature on page 161 and then turn to the map and caption on page 159. Using information from both sources, have students locate on the map the Outer Banks, Roanoke Island, breakers, breaches in the Outer Banks. Ask: Why might the ships have sunk? *(as a result of a northeaster)* Why is there a sea creature in the water? *(It illustrates how perilous the sea was thought to be.)* VISUALIZING

Meeting Individual Needs
Reteaching

Encourage students to pause after reading sections of the text and retell in their own words the "stories." For example, have students read from the bottom of page 157 to the top of page 159. The section is about the colony on Roanoke Island. Ask students: Why is it called the "Lost Colony"? What could have happened there?

An Armada Is a Fleet of Ships

Led by Sir Francis Drake, England defended itself against powerful Spain. The English, the underdog in the sea battle, defeated the Spanish Armada. The victory set the stage for England and France to step up their colonization of North America in the 1600s. Once again, America's population would become more diverse.

ASK

1. Why was Sir Francis Drake a hero to the English? *(Drake was the first captain to sail a ship around the world; he stole fortunes from the Spanish; brought great treasure and spices back to the queen.)* How did the queen show her appreciation? *(by making him a knight)*

2. Why did the Spanish say that Drake was a "master-thief?" *(Drake stole fortunes from Spanish ships, captured silver on land, raided ports, and burned their towns.)*

3. What tactics, or methods, did the English use to defeat the Spanish Armada? *(They made a sneak attack, sent ships to set fire to the Armada, and used small, fast ships to fight the big Spanish galleons.)*

4. Have students answer questions about the Armada on Resource 14 (TG page 86).

🌀 Ponder

Why did everyone predict that England would lose in its encounter with Spain? What is there to be learned from the story of the Spanish Armada?

✔️ Question Chart

DISCUSS

1. Some Englishmen said that England had the right to steal from Spain because Spain had stolen from the Indians. What would England have done if it were actually concerned about Indian property? *(returned the treasure to the Indians)* How did the argument about "stealing rights" serve the goals of the English? *(It justified their goal, which was to get Spain's gold.)*

2. What is your opinion of Drake's skills as a privateer, navigator, and naval commander? Explain. *(Responses will vary. Drake excelled in all areas.)*

WRITE

Divide the class into pairs. One student, a reporter for an English newspaper, will write about Drake's capture of the gold. The other student, a reporter for a Spanish newspaper, reports on the same event. Both students should provide headlines for their articles.

L I T E R A C Y   L I N K S

Words to Discuss

isthmus   armada

Ask students to use context clues to define the words. Then ask them to use the World Political map on page 178 to locate the Isthmus of Panama.

Reading Skills
Comparing and Contrasting

Have students brainstorm a list of Drake's qualities by finding examples of his actions and words that describe his attitudes or actions. Then ask students to list antonyms that describe these qualities *(loyal/hateful; fearless/terrifying; determined/relentless; avaricious/honest)*. Have students explain each word pair. *(He must have loved gold and money; he also turned over his loot to the queen.)* INFERRING

Skills Connection
Geography

Display the classroom world map and have students trace Sir Francis Drake's voyage as described in the text. Then have them locate Cadiz, Spain, and the Netherlands. Have them find the English Channel, and explain that the channel was the destination of the Spanish Armada and the location of the great sea battles between England and Spain.

The End: Keep Reading

In 1600, most of North America still belonged to the Indians. But along the fringes of North America were land-hungry Europeans. They were ready to write new chapters in the history of this hemisphere.

ASK

1. If you soared across America in 1600, what would the human population look like? *(There were diverse Indian populations, and small groups of European newcomers in Florida, New Mexico, and New France.)*

2. What conditions in England might push people toward North America? *(poverty, overcrowding, crime, desire to earn a profit, and so on)*

DISCUSS

1. What event will change the human face of North America in the 1600s? *(The English will start a colony in North America, which will eventually grow into the United States.)*

2. Discuss with students what they know about the fate of the First Americans in the 17th and 18th centuries. *(Responses will vary. Native populations were drastically reduced by both conflict and disease.)* Would it have been any different if the Spanish Armada had successfully defeated the English? *(Based on Spain's past behavior, it would not have been different.)*

**Ponder**
Suppose students in the future enter a time capsule and fly over the United States in the 21st century. What will they think?

✓ Question Chart

WRITE

Suppose you could send a message back in time to the early European settlers. What advice or warnings would you give them? What encouragement would you give them? What amazing landform would you tell them to look for? Write your message in the form of a letter.

LITERACY LINKS

Words to Discuss

rampant

Share with students that *rampant* means "widespread." Then ask students to name words they have learned in Book 1 that help them understand history. List on the board students' words for the class to review and discuss.

Reading Skills
Analyzing Rhetorical Devices

Ask: Why does the author ask readers to ride in a time capsule to take a look at America? *(to "see" and "hear" for themselves what they've read about; to get a glimpse of the changes that have taken place)* Why is this a good way for the author to end this book? *(The author has used the idea of a time capsule before, in the opening chapters, so it connects readers to the beginning of the story of the First Americans.)*
CONNECTING

Skills Connection
Geography

Have students look at the Resources map on page 183 and the front endpaper map of the locations of Native Americans in 1600. Ask students to predict how colonization will affect these people and resources.

THINKING ABOUT THE THEMES

The following questions will help students relate the book's themes to the content of Part 7. You may wish to use the questions for classroom discussion or have students answer them in written form.

1. What events and ideas in England and France help to explain the movement of their people to the Americas? *(religious persecution and conflicts, the competition for wealth and power sparked by Spanish conquest, the wish to establish new, more perfect societies)*

2. Since the Ice Age, the First Americans had adapted to new environments as they moved throughout the continent. How will the ability to adapt affect the Europeans in America? *(If they can learn how to survive in the New World, Europeans will eventually move into all parts of the Americas.)* How successful have the Europeans been in adapting to the New World so far? Explain. *(Most of their settlements have failed; they have trouble getting food and getting along with the Native Americans.)*

3. Have students complete the timeline of exploration on Resource 15 (TG Page 87).

4. Draw students' attention to the other themes that have been posted around the room. Give them the opportunity to explore the relevance of these themes to Part 7. Accept choices that are supported by sound reasoning.

ASSESSING PART 7

Use Check-Up 7 (TG page 71) to assess student learning.

NOTE FROM JOY HAKIM

It is the ability to order the world into meaningful patterns or stories that makes for great creative intellect. Good minds see connections. That is the skill we need to develop in our students.

PROJECTS AND ACTIVITIES

▶ A Queen's Party

Ask students to work in small groups to write and act out a play. The setting is a state dinner hosted by Queen Elizabeth in honor of Sir Francis Drake, who she has just knighted. Each guest at the party will make a toast, or a short speech, that honors either Drake or the queen.

▶ Proposal for a Colony

Have students work in small groups to write a proposal which they present their plans for an English colony to Queen Elizabeth. They should include their ideas for a good society, along with an understanding of the problems of setting up a community in the American wilderness.

▶ The Armada in Song and Verse

Have students write a poem or lyrics for a song about the defeat of the Spanish Armada. Encourage some students to compose their piece from the point of view of a Spanish writer.

▶ Style in the Elizabethan Age

Have students look at the illustrations that show the Elizabethan style of dress. Ask them to create a portrait gallery of historical figures, such as Queen Elizabeth, William Shakespeare, Walter Raleigh, and Francis Drake. They may photocopy the pictures, redraw them, or use other sources to create their gallery. When students display their portraits, have them point out features of Elizabethan clothing—for example the collars, ruffles, jewelry and so on.

★★ FACTS TO SHARE ★★

Many stories helped increase the superhero status of Sir Francis Drake. One story was that Drake beat a drum that had the power to give courage to his men as they went into battle. Another legend told of a magic mirror that showed Drake where every enemy ship could be found. It was also said that some Spanish sailors jumped overboard rather than face Drake, whom they called "The Dragon."

Name _____ Date _____

Check-Up 1

Answering these questions will help you understand and remember what you have read in Chapters 1-4. Write your answers on a separate sheet of paper.

1. What did Thomas Paine mean by "the Cause of America is . . . the Cause of all Mankind"?

2. Define each of these terms. Then tell how the term is important in a government that gets its authority from the people it governs.
   a. democracy
   b. Constitution
   c. Bill of Rights

3. Using each of the following place names, write a description of the journey of the First Americans to North America.
   a. Alaska
   b. Beringia
   c. Siberia

4. Explain how each of these time periods got its name.
   a. Ice Age
   b. Stone Age
   c. Iron Age

5. *Indian*, *Native American*, and *First American* are often considered synonyms. Explain the origin and meaning of each term.

6. Why did Beringia disappear? How did this affect the First Americans?

7. How did the disappearance of large animals affect the First Americans?

8. Suppose you were one of the first Native Americans to learn to ride a horse. Write a diary entry describing how this amazing animal has changed your life.

9. The First Americans had rich and varied cultures. Give details about their achievements in the following areas.
   a. farming
   b. hunting
   c. inventions
   d. housewares

10. Indicate the ages of these archaeological finds on the timeline. Label the timeline with the corresponding letters.
    a. Kennewick Man (Washington)
    b. Luzia (Brazil)
    c. Monte Verde tools (Chile)

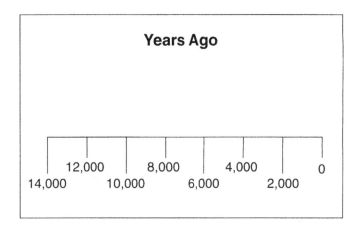

Years Ago

14,000   12,000   10,000   8,000   6,000   4,000   2,000   0

Name _____   Date _____

Check-Up 2

Answering these questions will help you understand and remember what you have read in Chapters 5-12. Write your answers on a separate sheet of paper.

1. What do the Eskimos call themselves? How did they get this name?

2. Why is each of the following places an important source of information about early Native Americans?
   a. Mesa Verde, Colorado
   b. Serpent Mound, Ohio
   c. Cahokia, Illinois

3. Define each of these terms. Tell which Native American group the term refers to.
   a. kiva
   b. potlatch
   c. nomads
   d. slash-and-burn farming

4. Name the people who lived in each type of house. Then explain how each type of building reflected the environment in which the people lived.
   a. igluviga
   b. pueblo
   c. wigwam
   d. longhouse

5. Which animal did the Plains Indians depend on most? How did they use this animal?

6. If you could jump aboard the author's time capsule and view the lands of the Mound Builders, what remarkable landmarks would you see? Give at least two examples. Describe each one.

7. Choose one Native American nation from this period that interests you. Write two paragraphs briefly describing this nation and telling the details that captured your attention.

8. What conflict did the Iroquois hope to end by forming a confederacy? What were some of the features of the confederacy?

9. Explain how climate and geography caused Native Americans to develop diverse societies. Give examples of this diversity.

10. Complete the chart by checking each box that applies to each Native American culture.

	Cliff Dwellers	Northwest Coast	Plains	Mound Builders	Eastern Woodlands
Farmers					
Hunter-Gatherers					
Traders					
Nomads					
Apartment Houses					
Wooden Houses					
Tepees					
Wigwams					

Name _____ Date _____

Check-Up 3

Answering these questions will help you understand and remember what you have
read in Chapters 13-20. Write your answers on a separate sheet of paper.

1. Each of the following people played a key role in events described in Chapters 13-20. Tell who each person was and what he did.
   a. Thorfin Karlsfeni
   b. Marco Polo
   c. Johannes Gutenberg
   d. Prince Henry
   e. Vasco Nuñez de Balboa

2. Explain where each of the following places is located. What was the significance of each place for European exploration?
   a. Vinland
   b. Lisbon
   c. San Salvador
   d. Strait of Magellan

3. Define the following terms. Explain why each was important to European exploration.
   a. movable type
   b. compass
   c. Indies

4. Imagine you are an archaeologist studying Viking exploration of North America. What mysteries would you like to solve? What sources would you use to solve them?

5. Why were 15th-century Europeans so interested in ocean exploration?

6. Answer these questions about Christopher Columbus and his explorations.
   a. What was he hoping to find?
   b. Which of his ideas were right? Which of his ideas were wrong?

7. Imagine the surprise the Taino felt on first seeing Columbus and his crew. Write a short message that runners might have delivered throughout their island.

8. Explain why our country is not called the "United States of Columbia."

9. What was the Columbian Exchange? Give some examples.

10. Organize the following events on the timeline according to the century in which they happened. (If events occurred in the same century, place them in time order in that century.) Label the timeline with the corresponding letters.
   a. Balboa sees the Pacific Ocean
   b. Marco Polo travels to China
   c. Columbus makes first voyage to America
   d. Cabot explores Newfoundland
   e. Magellan's ship sails around the world
   f. Gutenberg prints books with movable type

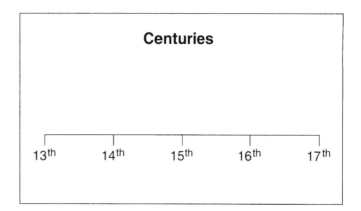

Centuries
13th   14th   15th   16th   17th

Name _____   Date _____

Check-Up 4

Answering these questions will help you understand and remember what you have
read in Chapters 21-24. Write your answers on a separate sheet of paper.

1. Suppose you are each of the following people.
   Describe your place in history. Begin with "I
   am _____, and I changed the world...."
   a. Martin Luther
   b. Hernando Cortés

2. Tell how each of the following pairs of terms
   is linked.
   a. Inquisition, Reformation
   b. smallpox, immunity
   c. colony, home country

3. Imagine you are one of Cortés's conquistadors
   seeing Tenochtitlán for the first time. Describe
   what you see, and compare it to Spanish
   cities.

4. History is full of "what ifs." Explain how the
   following "what ifs" would have changed
   history.
   a. What if the Aztecs had been immune to
      smallpox?
   b. What if 15th-century Europeans believed
      that all people could worship as they
      wished?
   c. What if Ponce de León had found gold in
      Florida?

5. How was Pizarro's conquest of the Incas
   similar to Cortés's conquest of the Aztecs?
   How was it different?

6. How did Europeans' religious beliefs influence
   their actions in the Americas?

7. What were some of the positive results of the
   Spanish conquest of the Aztec and Inca
   empires?

8. Explain this statement: The movement of
   Spaniards to the Americas made the
   population of the Americas more diverse and
   the population of native peoples less diverse.

9. Choose a leader from this period whom you
   would most like to interview. List five
   questions you would ask that person.

10. Use the Very Short History of Mesoamerica
    feature on page 108 to identify the locations
    of these ancient Mesoamerican civilizations.
    Shade the approximate locations of each
    civilization on the map, using the colors
    indicated.
    a. Teotihuacano (red)
    b. Zapotec/Mixtec (blue)
    c. Maya (green)
    d. Toltec (yellow)

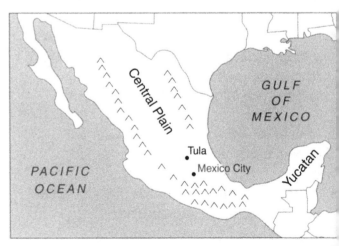

Name _____ Date _____

Check-Up 5

Answering these questions will help you understand and remember what you have read in Chapters 25-29. Write your answers on a separate sheet of paper.

1. The people below played key roles in the Spanish colonization of the Americas. Identify what each person did.
   a. Estebán
   b. Fray Marcos
   c. Bartolomé de Las Casas

2. How did the discoveries in Cuzco and Tenochtitlán influence the search for Cíbola and El Dorado?

3. Define each of these terms. Then explain whether it refers to the Spaniards or Native Americans.
   a. maize
   b. guerrilla
   c. missionary

4. Why did the Indians tell the Spaniards about "golden cities" that were just a few days ahead?

5. Why did the Spanish scholar Sepulveda believe that it was right to enslave Indians?

6. Narvaez and De Soto both led expeditions to Florida. Describe what happened to their expeditions.

7. The exploration of California by Europeans began with Alarcón and Cabrillo. What lands did each man reach or discover?

8. In what way was Coronado like other conquistadors? How was he different?

9. Where is Santa Fe located? Why is it an important city?

10. In the chart, write the future state or region of the United States that each person explored, a short description of the geography of that region, and the types of Indians that lived there.

Explorer	State/Region	Geography	Type of Indians
Coronado			
Cabrillo			
De Soto			

Name _____   Date _____

Check-Up 6

Answering these questions will help you understand and remember what you have read in Chapters 30-34. Write your answers on a separate sheet of paper.

1. Describe what the Spaniards accomplished in the Americas between 1492 and 1542.

2. These people had roles in the settlement of New France. Why was each person important?
   a. Giovanni da Verrazano
   b. Jacques Cartier
   c. Jean Ribaut
   d. Samuel de Champlain
   e. Jacques Marquette and Louis Joliet
   f. Sieur de la Salle

3. In the 16th century, what country was considered the most powerful in Europe? What would cause its decline?

4. Define each of these terms. Then tell why the term was important in the European settlement of North America.
   a. privateer
   b. galleon
   c. Northwest Passage
   d. black robes

5. Explain what role each of these places had in the European rivalry over North America.
   a. Straits of Florida
   b. St. Augustine
   c. Fort Caroline

6. Why did Spain, France, and England take such an interest in Florida?

7. As one of the women rulers in Part 6—Queen Isabella, Queen Mary I, or Queen Elizabeth I—

complete this sentence: I, _____, influenced world history by. . . .

8. Some nations considered privateers to be heroes, while other nations thought they were pirates. Choose a side and explain your view.

9. How did the French adapt to life in North America?

10. Show where the French did each of the following economic activities in North America. Make up a symbol for each activity, and place it in the correct places on the map.
   a. beaver trapping
   b. trade with Indians
   c. piracy
   d. fishing

Name _____ Date _____

Check-Up 7

Answering these questions will help you understand and remember what you have
read in Chapters 35-39. Write your answers on a separate sheet of paper.

1. What was so "Elizabethan" about England
during Queen Elizabeth's rule? How did the
queen set the tone of the times?

2. The following people played key roles in the
Elizabethan Age. Identify each person and tell
why he was important.
   a. Sir Humphrey Gilbert
   b. Sir Thomas More
   c. Sir Walter Raleigh

3. Define each of these terms. Then tell how the
term was related to England's dreams for
America.
   a. royal charter
   b. grant
   c. utopia

4. Why was Sir Francis Drake considered
England's hero?

5. What happened when the Spanish armada
fought the English navy?

6. How did England's position in the world
change after 1588?

7. What was the London Company?

8. English colonists landed in Roanoke late in the
spring of 1587. How did this contribute to the
failure of their settlement?

9. Why was John White so interested in the
success of the Virginia settlement?

10. The map shows three early European
settlements in North America. On the map,
label each site with its name and year of
settlement.

Name _____ Date _____

Resource 1

QUESTION CHART: *THE FIRST AMERICANS*

★ What were the major events?

_____ _____
_____ _____
_____ _____
_____ _____
_____ _____
_____ _____

★ Who were the significant people?

_____ _____
_____ _____
_____ _____
_____ _____
_____ _____

★ What were the important ideas?

_____
_____
_____
_____
_____
_____

Name _____ Date _____

Resource 2

ICE AGE MAP

Directions   Use information you have learned about the migration of peoples during the Ice Age to complete the map.

- Label **Beringia** and present-day **Alaska** and **Canada.**
- Use **arrows** to show land routes the First Americans may have used to migrate to North America.
- Draw **boats** to show how First Americans may have migrated across the sea.
- Draw **pictures** of animals that First American hunters followed.

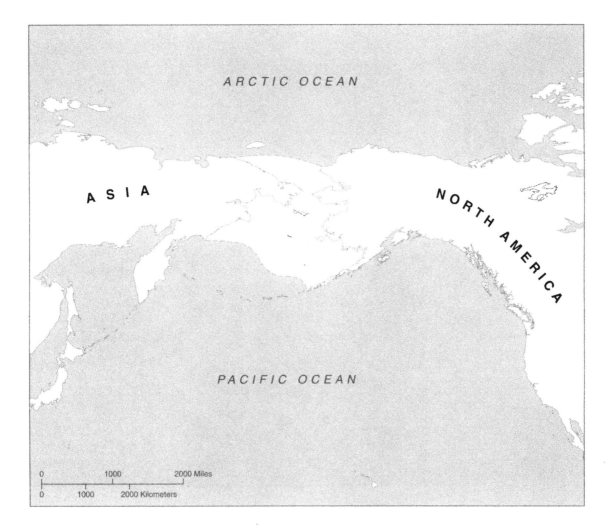

Resource 3

FIRST AMERICAN CULTURES

Directions   On the map, label the general locations of these Native American cultures: *Inuit, Northwest Coast, Anasazi, Plains, Mound Builders, Eastern Woodlands, Iroquois.* Underneath each label, draw a picture representing a characteristic of that culture. Use different-colored pencils to color in the approximate area that each of the peoples occupied.

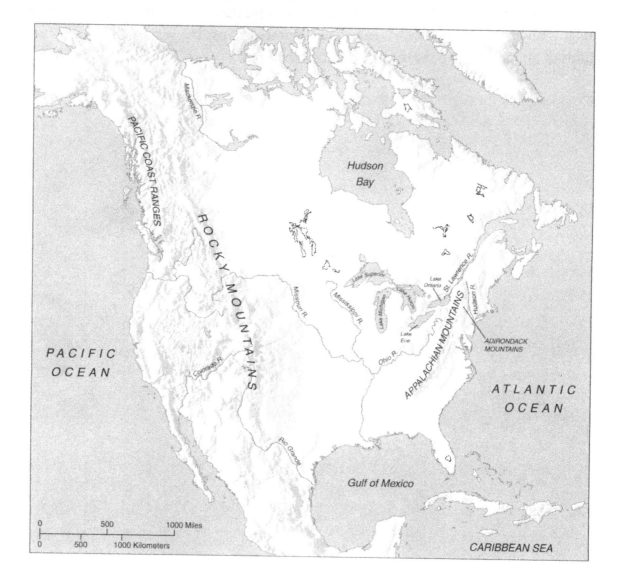

Resource 4

USING AN OUTLINE

Making an outline is one way that you can organize information so you can remember the main ideas and details of nonfiction writing. Most outlines follow this general form:

Subject *(This can be a sentence describing the subject or a title.)*

    I. Main idea about the subject
       A. Supporting detail
       B. Supporting detail
       C. Supporting detail
    II. Main idea about the subject
       A. Supporting detail
       B. Supporting detail
       C. Supporting detail

Here are two paragraphs from pages 48-49 of *The First Americans*. They give information about the Mound Builders culture. The paragraphs are followed by a sample outline highlighting the main ideas and details of the paragraphs.

We know quite a bit about some Mound Builders because of a 19th-century farmer named M. C. Hopewell. Hopewell found 30 mounds on his farm in Ohio. He had archaeologists dig carefully into them. Archaeologists are scientists who are trained diggers. From pieces of pots and bones and throwaway things they can tell a lot about the past. Historians would be lost without archaeologists.

The archaeologists on the Hopewell farm found more than just old pots and bones. They found copper, pearls, shells, mica, soapstone, and obsidian. They found teeth from sharks and teeth from grizzly bears. Most of these things had come from far away: the shells from the Atlantic coast, the obsidian from the Far West, the copper from mines near Lake Superior. So we know the Mound Builders were great traders; we think they used a kind of relay system to get goods to and from distant places. Their sophisticated culture was flourishing at the time when Jesus lived. (When was that?)

We know a lot about some Mount Builders.
  I. How we know
    A. 19th-century Ohio farmer named M. C. Hopewell found 30 mounds on farm.
    B. Archaeologists dug carefully into mounds.
    C. Archaeologists can tell a lot about past from what they dig up.
  II. What was found
    A. Copper, pearls, shells, mica, soapstone, obsidian were found.
    B. Teeth from sharks, teeth from grizzly bears were found.
    C. These things came from far away: Atlantic coast, Far West, Lake Superior.
  III. What these things say about Mound Builders
    A. They were great traders.
    B. They had a sophisticated culture.

Name _____ Date _____

Directions Use the instructions and sample outline on the previous page to write an outline for the following description of Cahokia from page 50 of *The First Americans.*

Now let's fly in our capsule, through a thousand years of time, to the year 1000, until we reach the Indian city of Cahokia. We are near three great rivers: the Mississippi, the Missouri, and the Illinois. This is a marvelous spot for a trading people to place a city. (Someday a city named St. Louis will sit across the Mississippi from here.)

Do you see the mounds? That's a foolish question—you can't miss them. One Cahokian mound is as tall as a 10-story building. Its base is broader than that of any of the pyramids in Egypt. The mounds look like flat-topped pyramids with temples and public buildings and statues on their summits. All those people in the streets are going to markets and schools and businesses.

Cahokia covers six square miles. About 25,000 people live here; another 25,000 people live in nearby villages.

Cahokia isn't a democracy; it is a slave society with a powerful ruler who is called the "Great Sun." He is thought to be the earthly brother of the heavenly sun.

Subject: _____

I. Located near three great rivers

   A. _____

   B. _____

   C. _____

II. Description of mounds and city
   A. One mound is as tall as 10-story building.

   B. _____

   C. _____

   D. _____

III. Size and population

   A. _____

   B. _____

IV. Government

   A. _____

   B. _____

   C. _____

Resource 5

NATIVE AMERICAN CULTURES

Directions   Complete the chart by writing details about each Native American culture group. Some examples are given. Then, on a separate sheet of paper, write a short paragraph telling which culture interests you the most, and why.

Culture Group	Houses/Buildings	Ways to Get Food/ Important Animals and Crops	Religion/ Social Structure/ Government	Customs/Arts/ Inventions
Inuit	igluviga			
Anasazi		farming		
Plains				
Northwest Coast				potlatch
Mound Builders			"Great Sun"	
Eastern Woodlands	wigwam			
Iroquois				

Resource 6

INTERPRETING PRIMARY SOURCES

A primary source is information about an event made by someone who was present when the event took place. Here are some examples of primary sources:

- journals or diaries by eyewitnesses
- newspaper accounts of events
- television or radio reports

Historians use primary sources to help readers feel that they are present when something happened. Primary sources also tell us about the attitudes and ideas of the people who wrote them.

Directions   Read the following record of Columbus's first two days in America and his meeting with the Taino. The log was recorded by the son of a sailor in Columbus's crew. Then answer the questions.

From the log of the voyage of Columbus, 1492
I saw some with scars of wounds upon their bodies, and asked by signs the cause of them. They answered me in the same way that there came people from other islands in the neighborhood with the intention of seizing them. . . . It appears to me that the people are ingenious and would be good servants, and I am of [the] opinion that they would very readily become Christians, as they appear to have no religion. They very quickly learn such words as are spoken to them. If it please our Lord, I intend at my return to carry home six of them to your Highnesses, that they may learn our language.

1. From whose point of view are the Taino people described?

_____

2. How might communicating in sign language leave room for misunderstanding?

_____

_____

3. What are Columbus's plans for the Taino? What must Columbus have assumed in order to think his plans would work?

_____

_____

4. What does the last sentence imply?

_____

_____

Name _____ Date _____

Resource 7

THE COLUMBIAN EXCHANGE

Directions   Use information you have learned about the Columbian Exchange to fill in this chart. Then answer the questions below.

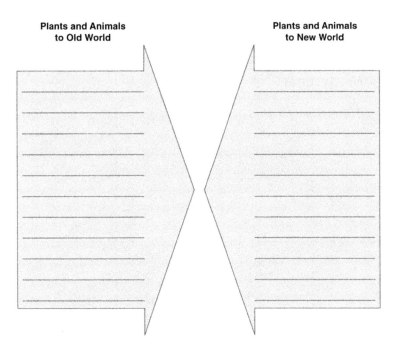

Plants and Animals
to Old World

Plants and Animals
to New World

1. Name things from both sides of the chart that you use today.

_____

_____

_____

2. Name two things the Old World got from the New World that you think were most important. Explain why.

_____

_____

_____

3. Name two things the New World got from the Old World that you think were most important. Explain why.

_____

_____

_____

Name

Date

Resource 8

CONQUEST OF THE AZTEC AND INCA

Directions   Complete the chart below about the Aztec and Inca civilizations at the time of the Spanish conquest. Some examples are included.

	Aztec	Inca
Native leader and government	Moctezuma	
Location		
Achievements		
Religious beliefs		worshiped gods
Source of wealth		
Leader and date of Spanish conquest		
Effect of conflict with Spanish		
Gains for Spain		

Resource 9

ANCIENT CIVILIZATIONS MAP

Directions On the map, label the general locations of these civilizations: *Aztec, Inca, Maya, Olmec, Mixtec, Toltec, Zapotec.* Use different colored pencils to color the approximate areas occupied by each people. Draw and label pictures representing characteristics of the cultures.

Name _____   Date _____

Resource 10

BIOGRAPHICAL PROFILE OF ESTEBÁN

Directions Esteban is a fascinating historical figure. Make a biographical profile for him by completing the chart. Include dates that you know or can estimate.

Birthplace	
Arrival in America	
Experience in Florida	
Contact with Indians	
Travels in North America	
Exploration Leader	
Personality/Appearance	
Skills/Languages Spoken	
Death	

Resource 11

SPANISH EXPLORERS AND EXPEDITIONS

Directions   In the map legend, write the name of the explorer who followed each route shown on the map: *De Soto, Coronado, Fray Marcos and Estebán*. Then use information from Chapters 25-27 to complete the chart. Use another sheet of paper if necessary.

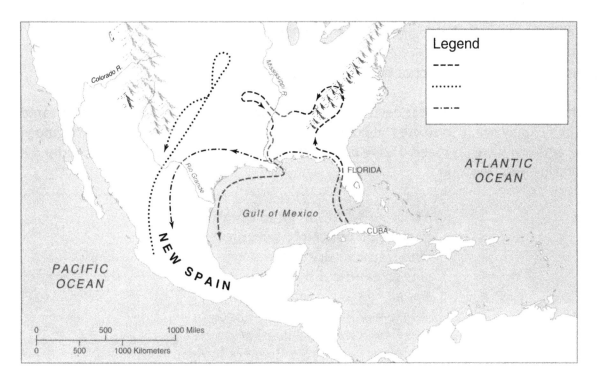

	De Soto	Coronado	Fray Marcos and Estebán
Year and place journey began			
Reason for journey			
People traveling on journey			
Places traveled			
How journey ended			

Resource 12

FLORIDA: WHO SHOULD YOU BELIEVE?

Directions On a separate sheet of paper, create a poster encouraging Huguenots to join Jean Ribaut's expedition to settle Florida. Include the following details:

- an exciting title
- words and pictures that make Florida seem like a good place to settle
- praise for Jean Ribaut
- a promise that Huguenots will not be persecuted in Florida

When you have finished your poster, read the following poem by Nicolas Le Challeux, a carpenter who joined Ribaut's expedition. (He wrote the poem after he returned to France.) Then, imagine you are Le Challeux, and you have just seen a copy of the Florida poster. On the lines below, write a letter to the editor stating your reaction.

> Whoever wishes to go to Florida,
> May he go where I have been,
> And return as dry and arid,
> and as worn out by rot.
> For all I have brought back
> A lovely white stick in my hand.
> But I am alive not defeated:
> It is time to eat; I am dying of hunger.

_____

_____

_____

_____

_____

_____

_____

_____

_____

_____

_____

_____

Resource 13

OBSTACLES TO EUROPEAN SETTLEMENT OF FLORIDA

Directions   Complete the web by including details from Chapters 32-33 that explain the obstacles various European nations faced in settling Florida. Include dates of conflicts when possible.

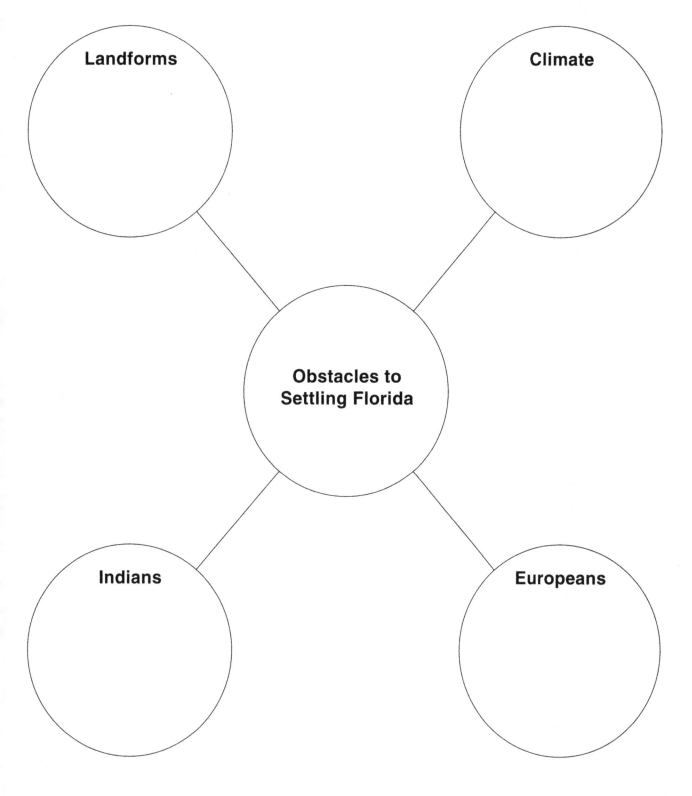

Resource 14

THE SPANISH ARMADA

Directions   Read the following report of the opening battle between the Spanish Armada and the British fleet from the July 23, 1588 issue of the *English Mercurie*. This report was published two days after the battle occurred. Then, using what you learned in Chapter 38 and this excerpt, answer the questions below.

On the 20th Capt. Fleming, who had been ordered to cruise in . . . the Channel . . . brought advice . . . that he had seen the Spanish Armada . . . making for the entrance of the Channel with a favorable gale. Though this intelligence was not received till near four in the afternoon, . . . the *Ark-Royal*, with five of the largest frigates, anchored out of the harbor that very evening.

The next morning, the greatest part of her Majesty's fleet got out to them. They made in all about eighty sail, divided into four squadrons, commanded by Lord High Admiral Howard in person, Sir Francis Drake Vice-Admiral, and the Rear-Admirals Hawkins and Forbisher. But about one in the afternoon, they came in sight of the Spanish Armada . . . sailing in the form of a half-moon, the points whereof were seven leagues [about 21 miles] apart.

By the best computation . . . they cannot be fewer than one hundred and fifty ships of all sorts; and several of them called galleons . . . are of a size never seen before in our seas, and appear on the surface of the water like floating castles. . . . The Lord High Admiral . . . directed the signal of battle to be hung out. We attacked the enemy's rear with the advantage of the wind. The Earl of Cumberland in the *Defiance* gave the first fire; My Lord Howard himself was next engaged for about three hours with Don Alphonso de Leyva in the *St. Jaques*, which would certainly have surrendered, if she had not been . . . rescued by Ango de Moncada.

In the meantime, Sir Francis Drake and the two Rear-Admirals Hawkins and Forbisher vigorously bombarded the enemy's rearmost ships . . . , which were forced to retreat much shattered to the main body of their fleet. . . .

About sunset we had the pleasure of seeing this invincible Armada fill all their sails to get away from us. The Lord Admiral slackened his, in order to expect the arrival of twenty fresh frigates, with which he intends to pursue the enemy, whom we hope by the grace of God to prevent from landing one man on English ground.

1. Compare the size and number of the ships in the two fleets.

_____

2. Who were the British commanders?

_____

3. Why was it important for the British to attack the enemy "with the advantage of the wind"?

_____

4. About how long did this battle last? What was the result?

_____

Name _____ Date _____

Resource 15

TIMELINE OF EUROPEAN EXPLORATION AFTER COLUMBUS

Directions Complete the timeline of European exploration by writing in details about an exploration or settlement for each of the dates.

1492 _____

1497 _____

1507 Amerigo Vespucci reaches South America.

1513 Ponce de León explores Florida.

1513 _____

1519 _____

1525 Verrazzano finds the Hudson River.

1532 _____

1534 _____

1536 Estebán and Fray Marcos search for Cíbola.

1539 _____

1540 _____

1542 Cabrillo reaches California.

1587 _____

1598 _____

1608 _____

1610 _____

ANSWER KEY

CHECK-UP 1

1. He meant that freedom—the main cause of America—is really the goal for all people.
2. (a) a system of government that makes its leaders responsible to the people (b) the document that outlines the U.S. plan of government and provides a system of laws for the nation (c) the first 10 amendments to the Constitution which protect the people's basic rights
3. Possible response: Some of the First Americans came from *Siberia* during the Ice Age. They entered *Alaska* by crossing *Beringia*, the earth bridge that then existed between the continents of Asia and North America.
4. (a) Glaciers covered much of the earth. (b) Most tools were made of stone. (c) People learned to work in iron.
5. *Indian* was a name mistakenly given to the people of America whom Columbus met. *Native Americans* suggests that these people originated here. *First Americans* implies that these were the first people to come here. All the terms indicate that these people have been in America for a very long time.
6. The climate got warmer, the glaciers melted, and the oceans rose, covering the Beringia land bridge. North America was cut off from Asia; no new people or animals could come from Asia, and none could go back to Asia. The First Americans developed cultures independent of their Asian cousins.
7. First Americans adopted different lifestyles when the large animals disappeared: they turned to farming, gathering, trading, and hunting smaller game.
8. Diary entries should mention the speed of the horse, making it easier to hunt and travel long distances.
9. (a) They developed corn, potatoes, and other vegetables; made chocolate, grew peppers and tomatoes, and learned how to cure sickness with plants and herbs. (b) They worked together to drive animals into ditches and bogs and speared them; made flint spears and invented the atlatl. (c)They made precise calendars, invented the hammock, canoe, and snowshoes, built pyramids temples, and cities. (d) They made beautiful jewelry, woven materials, and pottery.
10. (a) 9,000 years ago (b) 11,500 years ago (c) 33,000 years ago

CHECK-UP 2

1. Inuit; it was the Algonquin name for them, and means "eaters of raw flesh."
2. (a) The cliff dwellings give clues about the life of the Anasazi. (b) The mound shows the building skills and the power of the spiritual beliefs of the Mound Builders (c) Artifacts and remains of temple mounds tell us about the Mississippian culture.

3. (a) round room dug into ground of a pueblo; meeting place to make laws, practice religion, or socialize; Anasazi and Pueblo (b) extravagant parties; illustrated the wealth c class-oriented societies of peoples; Northwest Coast (c) people who move around from place to place, usually following migrating animals; Plains Indians (d) method of farming in which trees are cleared, brush is burned, and th ashes are hoed into the ground as fertilizer; Eastern Woodlands
4. (a) Inuit: used the snow and ice that covered the land (b Anasazi, Pueblo peoples: used the sun to bake clay bricks for building in the desert (c) Woodland Indians: built one-room houses with forest materials (d) Iroquois: used forest materials to build large houses that fit several families
5. Buffalo; they used its meat for food; its skin to make their houses, clothes, shoes, rope, and wool; sinews for thread; bones for awls and tools; dung for fuel; bladders fc jugs and drinking containers.
6. earth mounds, both large and small; the Serpent Mounc a long, curvy mound in the shape of a snake, large, flat-topped pyramids
7. Responses will vary.
8. The Iroquois formed the confederacy to end the wars of vengeance between themselves; each nation had its own identity and laws; a council of all the tribes made importa decisions, such as matters of war; all decisions had to be unanimous.
9. The various Indian groups adapted to the different geographic and climatic conditions. For example, the Plains Indians lived in tepees, easily transported houses made from long sticks and buffalo hides, whereas the Eastern Woodland Indians built permanent homes from wood and other forest materials. The Anasazi learned how to farm in a dry area, whereas the Northwest Coast Indians took advantage of the abundance of the seas and forests for their food.
10. Cliff Dwellers: farmers, apartment houses; Northwest Coast: hunter-gatherers, traders, wooden houses; Plains: nomads, hunter-gatherers, tepees; Mound Builders: farmers, traders, wooden houses; Eastern Woodlands: farmers, traders, wigwams

CHECK-UP 3

1. (a) Viking who settled for a while in North America for a while (b) European who traveled to China in the 13th century (c) German whose printing press made Marco Polo's book a best-seller and encouraged people to try to reach Cathay (d) Portuguese prince in 15th century who promoted sailing, mapmaking, and ocean exploration; (e) Spanish explorer who was the first European to see the Pacific Ocean from America
2. (a) Newfoundland (Canada), North America; first European (Viking) settlement in America (b) Portugal; mad into a center of learning and interest in navigation by Prince Henry (c) first land in America claimed in the name

of Spain (by Columbus) (d) waterway at southern tip of South America through which Magellan passed to get to the Pacific Ocean

3. (a) A way of printing that made books available to many people; Europeans learned about China and became interested in exploration. (b) Device with a magnet pointing north; it helped navigators sail farther out to sea. (c) The European name for East Asia; the search for an ocean route to the Indies prompted the European discovery of the Americas.

4. Responses will vary, but should include finding out the dates and extent of various explorations, using evidence from zoology, archaeology, anthropology, and literature to help solve mysteries.

5. Their imaginations were fired by Marco Polo's book; they wanted to find better routes to the Indies; the overland routes to the East were dangerous and long; a new spirit of learning and exploration had flowered in Europe.

6. (a) a sea route to the Indies by sailing west from Europe (b) He was right in thinking he could get to the Far East by sailing west; he was wrong in thinking the Earth is a lot smaller than it really is.

7. Responses will vary, but should include descriptions of the boats, the sailors' skin and clothing, the odd way the newcomers talk and act, and so on.

8. Columbus thought he had reached the Far East, not that he had come upon an unknown continent. Amerigo Vespucci realized South America was a continent, and let people know about it. The mapmaker Martin Waldseemüller labeled the new continent with Vespucci's first name because Vespucci had written about the continent.

9. the movement of plants and animals between the "New World" and the "Old World"; any of the plants and animals mentioned on Student Book page 82.

10. (a) 16th century (b) 13th century (c) 15th century (d) 15th century (e) 16th century (f) 15th century

CHECK-UP 4

1. (a) by posting my 95 Theses, trying to reform the Catholic Church, and helping to create new Christian religions. (b) by conquering the Aztecs and beginning the Spanish domination of the Americas.

2. (a) The Inquisition, or the Spanish religious court that persecuted non-Catholics, was one reason the reformers wanted to change the Catholic church. (b) Most Spaniards had an immunity to smallpox, but Indians did not, and died from it. (c) A colony is a region controlled by a foreign country; the place where the colony's settlers come from is their home country.

3. Responses will vary.

4. (a) More Indians would have been left alive to resist the European conquistadors; the Indians might have defeated the Europeans or limited their conquests. (b) They might have had fewer religious wars, and might have dealt more

fairly with the Indians. (c) The Spanish might have placed more colonies in eastern North America, causing the United States to have a much stronger Spanish influence.

5. Both men led small armies with guns against much larger forces. Both captured and killed the leader of the civilization. Both destroyed the civilization and took its gold and silver. Pizarro and his soldiers defeated the Incas by themselves; Cortés had the help of neighboring tribes whom the Aztecs had conquered.

6. They believed that Catholicism was the only religion; they persecuted Indians, viewing them as terrible people who practiced human sacrifices as part of their belief system.

7. The Spaniards brought government and schools, and they built churches and palaces. They ended human sacrifices.

8. The Spaniards brought enslaved Africans to America, leading to intermarriages between Europeans, Africans, and Indians. After the Spaniards came, three quarters of the Indians in Mexico died from war and disease, and Indian peoples elsewhere met similar fates.

9. Responses will vary.

10. (a) the area of the Central Plain north of Mexico City (b) the central mountains south of Mexico City (c) the area from the Yucatan Peninsula on the Gulf of Mexico across to the Pacific Coast (d) around Mexico City

CHECK-UP 5

1. (a) African from Morocco who came to America as a slave, survived Narváez's expedition into Florida, went on an expedition to find Cíbola (b) priest from New Spain who searched for Cíbola and announced he'd found it (c) Spanish priest who freed his Native American slaves and lobbied for the rights of Indians

2. Cíbola and El Dorado were legendary cities of gold. The Spaniards had found so much gold in Cuzco and Tenochtitlán that they thought they would find gold the legendary cities to the north.

3. (a) corn, a staple Indian food (b) fighting with no organized lines, used by the Indians against the Spanish (c) person who goes out into the world to convert others; missionaries converted thousands of Indians, some of whom adopted Catholicism but still practiced their native religions.

4. to trick the Spaniards into going away

5. He said it was natural for some to be masters and some to be slaves and thought Indians were inferior to Europeans.

6. Narváez marched up and down Florida coast in horrible conditions, captured Apalachee village, killed many Indians, was killed by Indians. De Soto also landed in Florida, captured an Apalachee village; endured difficult marches in swamps and jungle, was ambushed by guerrillas, reached Mississippi River, died of fever.

7. Alarcón: sailed up the Gulf of California and into the Colorado River. He may have been the first European to reach California. Cabrillo sailed up the Pacific coast as far as San Diego bay in what is now California.

8. Like: good leader; wanted to find Cíbola; had well-equipped, well organized expedition; wore armor; rode horse; fought and killed Indians. Unlike: took more than 1,000 Mexican Indians; treated Indians well; took herds of cattle and sheep.

9. Santa Fe is located in what is now New Mexico in the southwest United States. It was the first permanent European colony in the North American West.

10. *Coronado*: northern Mexico and Southwest and plains of U.S.; mountains, canyons, dry lands, grasslands; Zuni, Pueblo. *Cabrillo*: west coast of Mexico and California; Pacific coast and mountains; California Indians. *De Soto*: Florida, Alabama, Southeast U.S. to the Mississippi River, Texas; swamps, rivers, marshes, bogs, bayous; Appalachees, Eastern Woodlands Indians.

CHECK-UP 6

1. The Spaniards conquered more territory than the Roman Empire, defeated determined Indian foes, created new nations, built great cities.

2. (a) Italian explorer who sailed for France; reached New York Harbor and Canada (b) French explorer who made three voyages to Newfoundland and New Brunswick (c) French explorer who tried to set up a French base in Florida (d) French explorer and trader; established Quebec and formed alliance with Algonquin and Huron Indians, but angered Iroquois (e) French priest and mapmaker who explored the upper Mississippi River (f) French noble who explored the entire Mississippi River

3. Spain was the most powerful European country, but all the gold and silver from America would mess up its economy, cause its industry to decline and inflation to increase. Peasants left for America. The Inquisition forced Muslims and Jews to leave and silenced religious free thinkers.

4. (a) a pirate ship in a nation's service (b) large, three-masted sailing ship (c) long sought-after water passage from the Atlantic to the Pacific through North America (d) name given to French missionaries by Native Americans

5. (a) passage taken by Spanish treasure ships to the Gulf Stream; where pirates and privateers gathered to rob them (b) Spanish base in Florida for protection of its fleet (c) French fort in Florida, captured by Spaniards, fought over by French, Spaniards, English, and Native Americans for next century

6. Florida was a strategic location because it was on the route of the Spanish treasure ships.

7. Students' responses should demonstrate knowledge of each monarch's achievements.

8. Heroes: They defend the religion and honor of their respective countries and increase the national wealth.

Pirates: They violate the right to private property and freeedom of the seas, they take what is not theirs.

9. by making friends with native peoples, and hunting and fishing as the natives did.

10. (a) throughout Canada (b) throughout Canada and down the Mississippi River valley (c) off the coast of Florida and the Carolinas (d) off the coast of Canada

CHECK-UP 7

1. Queen Elizabeth's energy, intelligence, and desire for new lands and power were reflected in the energy and desires of England's people.

2. (a) Englishman who held the first royal charter for the Americas (b) Englishman who wrote *Utopia* and influenced England's desire to create a good society (c) friend of Queen Elizabeth who sent the first three English expeditions to America

3. (a) legal document that outlined a plan for rights and government of a colony that was held by the proprietor (b) deed for land in America given to a proprietor by the monarch (c) the idea of a perfect society

4. He stole vast amounts of gold from the Spanish and brought it to England; he sailed around the world; he helped defeat the Spanish Armada.

5. The English defeated the Spanish because the faster British ships outmaneuvered the slower Spanish ships; English fire ships caused havoc amongst the Spanish; a storm wrecked most of the rest of the armada.

6. England became one of the most important powers in the world.

7. A business firm that sent Englishmen to America; the people it sent would begin the first permanent English colonies, which would grow into a new nation.

8. They landed too late to plant crops. John White went back to England to get supplies, but did not return for three years, and the colony was lost.

9. White had been in Raleigh's previous attempt to plant a colony in Virginia. His daughter and granddaughter were at Roanoke

10. From north to south: Quebec, in Canada, 1608; Roanoke in North Carolina, 1587; St. Augustine, in Florida, 1565

RESOURCE 1

Question Chart for use throughout the book.

RESOURCE 2

Maps should show Beringia, Canada, and Alaska labeled; an arrow pointing from Asia across the earth bridge to Alaska; an arrow pointing from Asia to North America through the Arctic Ocean; boats along the southern shore of the earth bridge. Pictures of animals may include mammoths and saber-tooth tigers.

RESOURCE 3

Maps should have *Inuit* labeled across northern Canada; *Northwest Coast* along the Pacific coast straddling the U.S.-Canadian border; *Anasazi* in the American Southwest; *Plains* east of the Rocky Mountains from Canada to Mexico; *Mound Builders* in the central U.S. on both sides of the Mississippi River; *Eastern Woodlands* in the eastern U.S. from southern New York southward. They may include *Iroquois* from east of the Great Lakes toward New England, *Apalachee* in Florida, and *Zuñi* in the American Southwest. Students' drawings should portray information mentioned in the text.

RESOURCE 4

I. A. Mississippi River B. Missouri River C. Illinois River II. A. One mound is as tall as 10-story building. B. Base is broader than any of the Egyptian pyramids. C. Look like flat-topped pyramids with buildings on top. D. People are going to markets and schools and businesses. III. A. City covers six square miles. B. 25,000 people live in city; another 25,000 live nearby. IV. A. not a democracy B. slave society with powerful ruler called "Great Sun" C. ruler thought to be earthly brother of the sun

RESOURCE 5

Inuit: igloos, pit houses; fishing, hunting seals, walrus, whales; religion unknown; kayak; *Anasazi:* cliff houses, apartment complexes, kivas; farming, growing corn, hunting deer, elk; had priests, no religious freedom, council leaders; weaving, potting, irrigation; *Plains:* tepees, earth-covered houses; hunting buffalo, some faming; had religions and traditions; skilled at using buffalo resources, traders; *Mound Builders:* mounds, temples, palaces, cities, pyramids; farming, corn; slave society in Cahokia; mound building; *Northwest Coast:* villages, houses made of wood; fishing, hunting-gathering, salmon, seals; class system, had slaves; potlatch, totem poles, singing, dancing; *Eastern Woodlands:* wigwams, villages; hunting-gathering with some farming, beans, corn, squash, squirrels; small tribes; tattooing, make-up, slash-and-burn farming; *Iroquois:* long houses, villages; farming with some hunting-gathering; confederacy, formed Iroquois league, sachems as leaders; creating stories, respect for women

RESOURCE 6

1. from Columbus's or a European perspective
2. Neither Columbus nor the Taino could be sure that the other was understanding the signs.
3. to make them into servants, to convert them to Christianity, to teach them Spanish; that the Taino would agree to his plans, that the Taino's own culture was not important to them

4. Possible response: Columbus seems to already imagine taking the Taino as slaves; he speaks of taking them to Spain as if they were sacks of flour.

RESOURCE 7

Plants and Animals to Old World: corn, potatoes, tomatoes, peppers, chocolate, vanilla, tobacco, beans, pumpkin, cassava, avocado, peanuts, cashews, pineapple, blueberries, quinine, sunflowers, wild rice, squashes, marigolds, petunias, turkey, sweet potatoes
Plants and Animals to New World: wheat, barley, oats, soybeans, sugarcane, onions, lettuce, okra, peaches, pears, watermelon, citrus fruit, rye, bananas, olives, chickpeas, oranges, horses, cattle, pigs, sheep, chickens, honey bees
1.-3. Responses will vary.

RESOURCE 8

Aztec: Moctezuma, kingdom; Tenochtitlán, Mexico; huge empire, exact calendar, beautiful city, canals, causeways, pyramids; belief in gods, human sacrifices to gods; vast supply of silver and gold, jade; Hernando Cortés, 1519; Aztec army defeated, Moctezuma taken hostage and dies, smallpox kills thousands of Aztecs; boatloads of silver and gold sent to Spain, Mexico City built on ruins of Tenochtitlán; gained control of Mexico. *Inca:* Atahualpa, empire; Cuzco, Peru; excellent roads, wonderful artwork and carvings in silver and gold; worshiped gods; extreme wealth in gold and silver; Francisco Pizarro, 1532; Atahualpa killed, many Incas killed, Cuzco conquered, silver and gold artifacts melted down into bars; gained riches and land.

RESOURCE 9

Students should label *Maya* under Chichén Itzá; *Zapotec* under Monte Alban, *Mixtec* under Mitla, *Toltec* under Tula, *Aztec* under Tenochtitlán, and *Inca* under Cuzco. Students should color Maya across the Yucatan Peninsula and to the Pacific coast; Aztec from Tenochtitlán to the Gulf of Mexico and in an area around Tenochtitlán; Inca throughout all of Peru; pictures will vary.

RESOURCE 10

Morocco, Africa; arrived as a slave in 1528 with Spanish explorer Narvaez; was one of four people who survived an Indian attack in Florida; captured by Indians in Texas, learned their languages; for 8 years walked from Texas to Mexico, staying with different peoples along the way; with Fray Marcos, led expedition that reached the Zuñi in America's southwest; friendly, liked to dance and sing, liked by Indians, wore Indian jewelry and feathers; healer, leader, knew Indian languages; killed by Zuñi after sending a gourd in friendship that the Zuñi thought was a symbol of war.

RESOURCE 11

De Soto: 1539, Florida; wealth and fame, find Cíbola, 500 Europeans, 2 women, Indian and African slaves; Florida, Alabama, Texas; De Soto dies of fever, about 300 people return after 4 years. *Coronado:* 1540, Compostela, Mexico; conquistadors, Fray Marcos, 300 Spaniards, some women, children, and Spaniards, 1,000 Indians; Arizona, New Mexico, Grand Canyon, Kansas; returned to Mexico after 2-year, 7,000-mile journey. *Fray Marcos and Estebán;* 1536, Mexico City; find Cíbola; explorers, 300 Indians; Texas, New Mexico; Estebán killed by Zuñi, Fray Marcos and men returned to Mexico City.

RESOURCE 12

Posters will vary, but should make Florida seem like a great place to settle. Letters to the editor should take the opposite viewpoint.

RESOURCE 13

Landforms: swamps, jungle; *Climate:* heat, storms, hurricanes that sank ships; *Indians:* murdered 5 Spanish priests and helpers in Chesapeake Bay; *Europeans:* In 1565 the Spanish attacked Fort Caroline and killed the French; Menendez murdered Ribaut and his men; French destroyed San Mateo in 1568; Drake attacked Spanish settlers in Santa Elena in 1586.

RESOURCE 14

1. The British fleet had about 80 ships; the Spanish fleet had about 150 ships. The Spanish ships were much larger than the British ships.

2. The British commanders were Lord High Admiral Howard, Vice-Admiral Sir Francis Drake, and Rear-Admirals Hawkins and Forbisher.

3. Since the ships used sails to move, having the advantage of the wind would be important to the fleet.

4. The battle lasted from about one in the afternoon to about sunset, or 7-8 hours.

RESOURCE 15

1492, Columbus reaches America. *1497,* John Cabot reaches Newfoundland. *1507,* Amerigo Vespucci reaches South America. *1513,* Ponce de León explores Florida. *1513,* Balboa sees the Pacific Ocean. *1519,* Cortés begins conquest of Aztecs. *1525,* Verrazzano finds the Hudson River. *1532,* Pizarro destroys the Inca Empire. *1534,* Cartier sails up the St. Lawrence River. *1536,* Estebán and Fray Marcos search for Cíbola. *1539,* De Soto lands in Florida. *1540,* Coronado sets out to search for Cíbola. *1542,* Cabrillo reaches California. *1587,* "Lost Colony" at Roanoke is founded. *1598,* Juan de Oñate settles New Mexico. *1608,* Champlain settles Quebec. *1610,* Santa Fe is founded.

CPSIA information can be obtained
at www.ICGtesting.com
Printed in the USA
BVHW021735170723
667296BV00003B/8